THE DEEP WORK SOCIETY
Book Three

The Book On
The Digital Reboot

How to Detox Your Mind Without Deleting
Your Life

The Book On Series
Anonymous

Published by The Book On Publishing, 2025.
First edition. June 22, 2025.

Website: https://thebookon.ca
Substack: https://thebookonpublishing.substack.com/

While every precaution has been taken in the preparation of this book, the publisher assumes no responsibility for errors or omissions, or damages resulting from the use of the information contained herein.

THE DIGITAL REBOOT: How to Detox Your Mind Without Deleting Your Life

First edition. June 22, 2025.

Written by Anonymous.

The Book On Series

The Book On Life Unscripted
The Book On Risk Management in Payments
The Book On AI for Everyday People
The Book On Relationships
The Book On Master The Algorithm
The Book On Saying No
The Book On Community Led Strategy
The Book On The Myth of Multitasking
The Book On The Burnout Blueprint
The Book On The Digital Reboot
The Book On The Shape of What's Coming
The Book On Strategic Obsession
The Book On High-Stakes Thinking
The Book On Artificial Leverage
The Book On Clarity
The Book On Uncertainty
The Book On Operational Excellence
The Book On Escape

Table of Contents

Read This First

This is not a book designed to entertain you. It's not here to charm, to soothe, or to hold your hand. It won't dazzle you with stories, metaphors, or motivational fluff. What you're having is a tool, an instruction manual written for people who are serious about learning, executing, and thinking at a higher level.

Every book in The Book On Series is built on a single premise: clarity beats complexity. We believe that when you strip away the noise, the emotions, the marketing spin, and the cultural rituals of "self-help," what's left is raw, unembellished instruction. That's what these books offer.

They are dry by design. Not because we don't care about language or narrative, but because when you're building something that matters, you don't need more distractions. You need a clear architecture. Mental scaffolding. Direction that respects your intelligence.

Each title in this series takes on a specific domain: decision-making, clarity, strategy, leverage, and uncertainty, and drills deep, not in sweeping generalizations, but in applied frameworks. These are books for builders, operators, founders, tacticians, and thinkers—people who don't just consume knowledge but operationalize it.

You'll find no chapter-long anecdotes here. No self-congratulatory memoirs. No bullet-point platitudes. Instead, what you'll get is structured insight: argument, example, application. The tone is direct. The prose is sober. The ideas are designed to be lifted out and used.

You won't be coddled, but you won't be misled either.

There's a place in the world for lyrical, emotional, story-driven books, and this isn't that place. This is a workspace. A blueprint. A conversation for people who are ready to act, not just absorb.

We respect your time and your intellect.

Welcome to The Book On Series.

Dedication

To the restless minds seeking stillness, to those
who crave presence beyond the screen, and to
everyone brave enough to reclaim their attention,
this book is for you.
- Anonymous

Epitaph

"To thine own self be true."
- William Shakespeare

Preface

Our phones are everywhere. They wake us in the morning, accompany us through the day, and often keep us company long after the world has gone quiet. They connect us, entertain us, inform us, and sometimes, they consume us.

If you've ever found yourself endlessly scrolling, checking notifications even when there's no real need, or feeling a creeping exhaustion despite "doing nothing," you're not alone. This book is for you.

The Digital Reboot isn't about quitting technology or becoming a digital hermit. It's not a guilt trip about screen time, nor a promise that deleting apps will magically fix your focus or peace of mind. Instead, it's a compassionate guide to reclaiming your attention, your energy, and your humanity in a world designed to pull you away from them.

This book grew from a simple recognition: our relationship with technology is complicated. It offers immense benefits, but these come with costs that we rarely see until they overwhelm us. The endless pings and scrolls don't just steal minutes, they erode our ability to think deeply, connect meaningfully, and rest fully.

But there is hope.

Across these pages, you'll find a path not just to detox but to reboot. To reset how you engage with your devices, your digital environment, and ultimately yourself. It's a journey of awareness, practical change, and gentle rewiring. It's about setting boundaries that stick, creating rituals that support focus, and building a digital life that serves your values rather than hijacking them.

Whether you're overwhelmed by work messages, distracted by social feeds, or simply tired of feeling at the mercy of your own devices, this book offers a way forward. You don't have to disconnect to feel whole; you have to reclaim control over the conditions that shape your mind.

The challenge is real, but so is your capacity to meet it. It won't always be easy, and it won't be perfect. But by the end of this journey, you may find something precious: the freedom to live fully, both online and off.

Welcome to *The Digital Reboot*. Let's begin.

Part I: The World in Your Pocket

Chapter 1: The Phone You Love Is Ruining You

Your phone is never far away. Whether it's in your pocket, on your desk, or resting face-up beside your bed, it feels like an extension of yourself. It carries your calendar, your contacts, your photos, and a constant stream of messages and updates. It's become an essential tool for work, socializing, entertainment, and even navigating your environment. Yet beneath this sense of familiarity lies a quiet but profound influence that few fully acknowledge.

The truth is that your phone is designed to capture and command your attention, shaping your thoughts and habits in subtle ways that you often don't notice. The companies behind these devices invest enormous resources into understanding how your brain works, using that knowledge to craft experiences that pull you back again and again. Every notification, every vibrating alert, and every red badge represents a carefully engineered signal, designed to trigger your brain's reward system and release small bursts of dopamine, the chemical linked to pleasure and reinforcement.

Your brain naturally craves novelty and unpredictability, and your phone leverages this instinct expertly. When you pick it up to check a single message or notification, you often find yourself swept into a cascade of content, posts, videos, and updates that can stretch for minutes or even hours without a clear stopping point. This pattern is not accidental; it is the product of sophisticated behavioural design that aims to keep you engaged as long as possible.

It is essential to understand that this is not a failure of willpower. The challenge is not about your self-control but about a system built to capture your attention. Our brains evolved in environments where sustained focus on a few tasks was essential for survival. They were not built to process the flood of fragmented information that digital technology now delivers. The relentless stream of pings and interruptions breaks your natural rhythms, splintering your attention and impairing your ability to think deeply or rest fully.

This constant state of distraction has tangible consequences. When you rapidly switch between apps, messages, and tasks, your brain must constantly reset itself, incurring a cognitive cost each time. This switching slows productivity, diminishes memory, and leads to increased mental fatigue. Instead of multitasking effectively, you are toggling between demands, which fragments your focus and drains your energy.

Moreover, your phone conditions you to expect ongoing stimulation, making periods of quiet or boredom increasingly uncomfortable. The absence of new notifications feels like a void to be filled, driving you back to the device to search for engagement even when you do not consciously desire it. This cycle reinforces itself, deepening dependence on your phone for relief from restlessness, yet simultaneously undermining your capacity for sustained attention.

Beyond productivity, this dynamic also affects your emotional and social well-being. The fragmented attention fostered by constant phone use reduces your ability to be fully present with the people around you. Conversations may become distracted or superficial, and moments of connection can slip by unnoticed. The paradox is that while technology promises connection, it often contributes to feelings of isolation and disconnection.

Recognizing these patterns is the first step toward change. Becoming aware of the ways your phone shapes your mind empowers you to reclaim your attention and your time. This is not a call to reject technology but to engage with it intentionally, setting boundaries that honour your needs rather than the demands of algorithms.

This book will guide you through that process, helping you rebuild a healthier relationship with your devices. You will learn how to understand the influence of digital design, create practical habits to protect your focus, and develop rituals that support presence and clarity. The goal is not to become a digital hermit but to become the architect of your attention.

Your phone is a powerful tool, but that power need not dominate your life. With conscious choices and thoughtful strategies, you can regain control over your digital environment and cultivate a mind capable of deep focus, rest, and meaningful connection.

This journey begins with seeing your phone as it truly is, not simply a friend or a convenience, but a complex force that can either serve you or consume you. From that clarity, you can build a new foundation for living well in the digital age.

Chapter 2: The Myth of Connection

In the early days of smartphones and social media, there was an undeniable promise: these tools would shrink the world, collapse distance, and bring people closer than ever before. A message could reach a friend across continents in seconds. Photographs and stories could be shared instantly. Conversations that once required planning and patience could happen spontaneously at any moment. The technology felt like magic, an unprecedented way to maintain and deepen our bonds.

But the reality is more complicated. Despite being more digitally "connected" than any previous generation, many people report feeling lonelier and more isolated. The explosion of social platforms, messaging apps, and online communities has not automatically translated into richer, more meaningful relationships. On the contrary, the digital age has often brought a paradoxical sense of disconnection.

The myth of connection lies in confusing availability with presence. To be connected means to be reachable or linked, a channel through which messages pass. But presence requires more. It requires full attention, emotional engagement, and genuine openness. True connection happens in moments where one person fully listens to another, where attention is given without distraction or hurry.

Online platforms, however, tend to reward speed and visibility rather than depth and presence. A quick like, a brief comment, or a rapid-fire exchange can make us feel involved and responsive, but often these interactions are surface-level. They create a buzz of activity without the substance of honest dialogue. Social media encourages broadcasting over listening, reaction over reflection.

This dynamic can erode our capacity for intimacy and empathy. Scrolling through curated images of friends' perfect moments can heighten feelings of inadequacy and loneliness. The endless comparisons and highlight reels obscure the messiness and complexity that make human relationships rich. It's easy to mistake the quantity of interactions for quality, but quantity alone cannot sustain emotional connection.

Moreover, the constant interruptions of notifications and pings fracture our attention during the moments we spend with others in real life. Even when sitting across from someone we care about, many find their minds elsewhere, pulled by the urge to check a phone or respond to a message. This divided attention diminishes the experience of being fully seen and heard, which is essential for trust and closeness.

It's important to understand that this isn't a simple matter of good or bad technology. Digital tools offer remarkable opportunities for connection, especially for those separated by distance, mobility issues, or social anxieties. They can provide support communities, access to information, and platforms for voices otherwise unheard.

The challenge is how to cultivate presence within and alongside these technologies. It means learning to use digital connections in ways that nurture rather than fragment attention. It means recognizing when online interactions enrich us and when they drain us. It means protecting the spaces where deep, focused listening and authentic exchange can happen, both online and offline.

Reclaiming connection in the digital age requires a conscious choice. It involves setting boundaries that allow for undistracted time with loved ones, being intentional about when and how to engage online, and cultivating habits that favour meaningful dialogue over reactive consumption. It asks us to value quality over quantity and depth over immediacy.

This chapter and the book that follows invite you to move beyond the myth that constant connectivity equals real connection. It encourages you to embrace presence as the true heart of a relationship. When you practice presence, your interactions deepen, your relationships strengthen, and you begin to experience connection in its most whole form, one that nourishes the mind, heart, and spirit.

Chapter 3: The Infinite Scroll Problem

The moment you unlock your phone and open specific apps, you enter a world without edges. Unlike a book with chapters or a website with pages, this digital space flows endlessly, posts, images, videos, and updates pour into view without pause, without clear stopping points. This is the infinite scroll, a design that promises endless discovery but often delivers something more complicated.

At first glance, infinite scroll feels like a gift. It lets you move seamlessly from one piece of content to the next without the friction of clicking "next" or waiting for pages to load. It offers an uninterrupted stream of information and entertainment tailored just for you. The promise is effortless browsing, the thrill of the unexpected, the joy of discovery.

Yet this design taps deeply into how our brains work, exploiting our innate desire for novelty and unpredictability. Each swipe holds the possibility of uncovering something surprising or rewarding. This uncertainty is a powerful lure. It activates the dopamine system, creating brief bursts of pleasure that encourage you to keep going.

What feels like a casual scroll quickly becomes a compulsive loop. Without natural stopping cues, the stream pulls you forward, making it difficult to disengage. The absence of clear breaks or endpoints removes the psychological signals that might otherwise tell you it's time to stop and reflect.

The consequences extend far beyond lost time. Infinite scroll rewires expectations and attention habits. When your mind is trained to move quickly from one snippet to the next, your capacity for sustained focus diminishes. You grow accustomed to shallow engagement, flitting from idea to idea without fully absorbing or processing any of them.

This fragmentation of attention carries a cognitive cost. Deep reading, thoughtful reflection, and creative thinking require uninterrupted mental space. The endless lure of new content makes these states harder to achieve. Your mind becomes restless, craving constant stimulation but rarely finding satisfaction.

In addition to undermining concentration, the infinite scroll generates mental noise. The stream is often filled with emotionally charged, sensational, or repetitive content designed to provoke reactions rather than encourage understanding. This flood of stimuli overloads your cognitive filters, making it harder to discern what is meaningful from what is merely distracting.

The experience can be paradoxical: overwhelmed by the volume of information yet bored by its lack of depth. The infinite scroll feeds a constant hunger for novelty while offering little nourishment. It encourages consumption without comprehension, participation without presence.

Recognizing the pull of infinite scroll is crucial. It's not merely a habit to break but a structural feature of many platforms designed to maximize your time on screen. Resisting it requires deliberate strategies that reclaim your agency.

In the chapters that follow, you will learn how to create boundaries that honour your brain's natural rhythms, how to cultivate practices that restore focus, and how to redesign your digital environment to prioritize quality over quantity.

Because the infinite scroll problem is not about your willpower failing, it's about understanding the architecture that shapes your behaviour and choosing how to navigate it with intention.

Breaking free from this cycle doesn't mean rejecting the digital world. It means reclaiming your right to pause, reflect, and choose what deserves your attention. When you learn to stop scrolling, you open space for more profound thought, richer experiences, and a more grounded life.

Chapter 4: We Built a Mirror, Not a Window

When social media first burst onto the scene, it was heralded as a revolutionary way to connect with the world, a digital window opening onto other lives, perspectives, and cultures. The promise was dazzling: an endless panorama of human experience, right at your fingertips, ready to broaden your horizons and deepen your understanding. Yet as the platforms evolved, a more complicated picture emerged. Instead of a window outward, many found themselves staring into a mirror.

This shift from outward connection to inward reflection is subtle but profound. The content you see isn't a neutral stream of information but one filtered, curated, and amplified by algorithms tuned to your behaviour, preferences, and past engagement. What this means is that instead of a broad view of the world, you are often shown a reflection of yourself, a digital echo chamber that reinforces your existing beliefs, emotions, and biases.

This is not merely an inconvenience. It has a profound psychological impact. When your digital environment acts like a mirror, it fractures your sense of identity and narrows your perception of reality. You begin to see your views and feelings magnified back at you, sometimes distorted, and you lose sight of alternative perspectives. Your world becomes smaller even as the screen's reach grows.

Social media encourages curation and performance. You present versions of yourself shaped by how you want to be seen, and in turn, you consume versions of others shaped by similar impulses. This dynamic creates layers of projection and expectation that blur authentic connection. The mirror doesn't just reflect; it amplifies insecurities and anxieties, fostering comparison and self-doubt.

The result is what some call the "shallowing effect," where the depth of our social and cognitive lives is reduced to brief, curated moments designed for maximum engagement rather than meaningful exchange. The mirror invites you to evaluate yourself constantly against an idealized standard, making it difficult to rest in your worth and complexity.

Beyond the personal, this inward turn has societal consequences. When communities are fragmented into echo chambers, polarization deepens, and shared understanding becomes more elusive. The digital mirror distorts public discourse, privileging outrage and reinforcement over nuance and empathy.

Recognizing that we have built mirrors, not windows, is essential for reclaiming a healthier digital life. It invites us to seek experiences that genuinely expand our horizons rather than reflect our existing selves. It challenges us to engage critically with the content we consume and the identities we perform online.

This awareness opens the door to new possibilities: cultivating curiosity instead of confirmation, embracing complexity instead of certainty, and seeking connection that transcends the screen's surface.

In the chapters ahead, you will discover strategies to break free from the mirror's hold, to find spaces of genuine openness, challenge your assumptions, and build a richer, more expansive digital life.

Because genuine connection, growth, and understanding require windows, not mirrors.

Chapter 5: The Shallowing Effect

As you navigate the digital landscape, you may begin to notice a peculiar change, not just in how you spend your time, but in how you think. The very tools designed to keep you connected and informed seem to be eroding your ability to engage deeply with ideas, with texts, and even with your thoughts. This is the shallowing effect, a quiet but powerful phenomenon shaping minds across the world.

It's not that information is scarce. On the contrary, we live in an era of unprecedented access to knowledge, stories, and perspectives. The challenge is not finding content but slowing down enough to absorb it meaningfully. Social media feeds, news cycles, and even streaming platforms bombard you with snippets, headlines, and rapid-fire updates that encourage a quick skim rather than thoughtful reflection.

The structure of these digital experiences favours brevity and immediacy. Attention is fragmented into bursts lasting seconds or minutes, punctuated by constant interruptions. The result is a cognitive environment that rewards speed over depth, breadth over focus, and surface-level engagement over sustained contemplation.

This environment reshapes your brain's habits. Your capacity for prolonged reading or concentration diminishes, replaced by a restless need for novelty and instant gratification. Long-form articles can be daunting, with complex ideas overwhelming, and reflective thinking a rarity. Your mental palate is saturated with fast bites but starved of rich nourishment.

The shallowing effect is not merely a consequence of technology but a consequence of how it's used and designed. Algorithms push content that maximizes clicks and shares, often favouring emotional extremes and simplicity over nuance. This creates feedback loops that further encourage quick reactions rather than slow understanding.

Beyond the intellectual impact, shallow engagement affects emotional and social realms as well. When you skim interactions or conversations, you miss the subtleties that foster empathy and connection. Relationships risk becoming transactional and superficial, lacking the depth that comes from truly being present with another person's experience.

Recognizing the shallowing effect is a crucial step toward reclaiming your cognitive life. It invites you to reconsider how and where you invest your attention, to seek out experiences that challenge your mind to slow down, to linger, and to grow.

The journey back to depth is neither swift nor straightforward. It requires patience, practice, and sometimes resistance to the pull of easy distraction. But it offers rewards beyond productivity: richer understanding, greater creativity, and a restored capacity to think clearly in a noisy world.

In the chapters ahead, you will explore practical ways to counteract shallow thinking, cultivate sustained attention, and build mental habits that support deeper engagement with the world and yourself.

Because in a world designed for speed, choosing depth is a radical act.

Chapter 6: Hyperstimulation Is the New Normal

It used to be that moments of quiet filled the gaps in your day. Waiting for a bus, sitting in a coffee shop alone, lying in bed before falling asleep, these used to be pauses, small windows where your thoughts could wander freely. These moments weren't empty; they were fertile. Your mind could process what had happened, imagine what might happen next, or rest.

But now, those same gaps are filled, instantly, reflexively, with screens. The moment your attention isn't demanded by something external, your hand reaches into your pocket: a few swipes, a new feed, a tiny burst of stimulation. Even the briefest idle moment is now an invitation to check something. You don't wait anymore; you scroll. You don't pause; you tap.

The result is a life without silence.

And without silence, your nervous system never really gets a break.

Hyperstimulation has become so normalized that we've stopped noticing it. We often take for granted that noise and input are ubiquitous, not just in the form of auditory noise, but also mental noise. Your senses are constantly flooded with colours, sounds, messages, and motion. It happens while you're working, relaxing, eating, or even walking. The line between attention and overstimulation has quietly blurred, until what used to be "a lot" now feels like the baseline.

But your body knows the difference, even if your mind doesn't always register it. It's not designed to process this much input, this often, this fast.

When your nervous system is constantly engaged, with the screen always lighting up, sounds chiming, and visuals moving, your body interprets this stream of stimulation as something to react to. Your heart rate ticks upward. Your breathing shallows. Your muscles tighten. The brain begins producing more stress hormones in response to the perceived demands. Over time, you start to live in a state of chronic activation. Not crisis, but not calm, either.

You may feel irritable without knowing why. Tired even after sleep. Anxious without an apparent trigger. These symptoms often aren't signs of mental illness or personality flaws. They're signs of an overstimulated system trying to keep up.

The irony is that we often reach for our devices to unwind. You might watch a show, scroll through Instagram, play a game, or reply to a few messages, thinking it's "downtime." And yet, your brain remains alert, tracking new content, scanning faces, reading tone, and interpreting cues. What we call relaxation is frequently just more stimulation, of a different flavour.

Hyperstimulation also affects memory. When you're constantly shifting from one input to the next, your brain has less opportunity to consolidate information. That's why entire days can pass in a blur. It's not that you weren't doing anything; it's that your experiences never had the chance to settle into long-term memory. The pace was too fast. There was no stillness to absorb what happened.

Creativity suffers, too. Original thinking doesn't come from speed or saturation. It comes from mental spaciousness. From wandering thoughts and gentle boredom. From letting your mind wander down a path without constant interruption. But when your day is saturated with digital noise, there's no room for the kind of boredom that births ideas.

Part of the challenge is that the world has trained us to equate stimulation with productivity, presence, even pleasure. We're conditioned to believe that if we're not doing something, especially something visible or digital, we're wasting time. But the truth is that mental rest, quiet focus, and non-reactive presence are essential for clarity, creativity, and well-being. Not occasional luxuries, but fundamental human needs.

To reclaim your mind, you have to reclaim your sensory space. That doesn't mean renouncing technology or fleeing the modern world. It means designing a new rhythm, one that allows for stretches of quiet, that doesn't fill every gap, that makes space for your nervous system to reset.

You can begin in small ways. Begin by shielding one part of your day from digital stimulation, such as the first hour after waking or the last before sleep. Notice how your body feels when it's not bouncing between notifications. Create zones in your home or times in your schedule that are screen-free, not as punishment, but as restoration.

The goal isn't to disconnect completely. The goal is to learn the difference between stimulation and nourishment. To notice what drains you and what restores you. To recognize that while the world might reward constant engagement, your body and brain are asking for something else.

Because hyperstimulation may be the new normal, but it doesn't have to be your normal.

Chapter 7: Digital Ghosts of Ourselves

There is a version of you that lives online, possibly several. You didn't set out to create these copies, but they emerged slowly, almost passively, every time you posted a photo, wrote a comment, liked a post, joined a platform, or updated a status. Over time, these traces accumulated, forming digital outlines that mimic your personality, preferences, and patterns. But while they resemble you, they are not you. They are projections. They are records. They are ghosts.

These digital selves don't age as you do. They don't forget, revise, or grow with you. A post from five years ago, a playlist from last summer, a bio you wrote in college, they still exist somewhere, long after you've moved on or changed. And for others, these fragments may be the only version of you they ever see. In some cases, your digital ghost feels more visible than your living presence.

This phenomenon creates a subtle tension. On the one hand, you control how these ghosts are formed. You choose what to share, how to curate your online identity, and how much of yourself to reveal. But at the same time, once those choices are made, the digital echo begins to live a life of its own. It is interpreted, recontextualized, and sometimes remembered in ways you never intended. You may move forward in your real life, but online, the past lingers indefinitely.

What complicates this further is the feedback loop between your digital self and your real one. The more you post, the more those posts are responded to. Likes, comments, shares, they all signal approval or interest. And even if you believe you're above the influence, your brain registers those signals. Your sense of identity begins to take shape around what others respond to. You start to shape your behaviour, perhaps unconsciously, to match the version of yourself that feels most validated online.

Eventually, it can become difficult to tell where your actual self ends and your digital self begins.

This divide isn't always harmful. There are times when digital expression offers safety, clarity, or access to parts of yourself you hadn't fully explored. But when the digital version begins to dominate, when it becomes the self you manage most carefully, it can distort your inner landscape. You may start to feel pressure to perform rather than exist. You may worry more about how a moment will look on camera than how it feels in your body. You may find yourself choosing what is shareable over what is meaningful.

This shift happens subtly. You start editing your life for visibility. Moments that could be savoured in solitude are filtered, captioned, and posted. Reactions start rolling in, and those reactions inform how you see the experience itself. Memory becomes shaped by response. Presence becomes mediated by documentation.

The danger here is not simply that you become performative, but that you begin to outsource too much of your self-understanding. If you constantly check how you're being perceived, liked, or shared, you erode the quiet confidence that grows in unobserved space. You start to rely on feedback from the crowd to confirm your identity. Without realizing it, your digital ghost begins to lead.

This isn't about shame or blame. It's about awareness. None of this means that sharing online is inherently wrong, or that building a presence is shallow. But it does mean asking whether the version of you that lives online reflects your inner life, or distracts from it. Whether you're shaping your digital self as an honest expression, or slowly bending to match a mould that feels safer, more acceptable, or more admired.

Your digital ghost is not going away. And perhaps it shouldn't. But you can choose how much power it holds. You can step back and examine which parts of your online presence feel true and which feel like masks. You can pause before posting and ask whether you're seeking connection or validation. You can consider whether your digital behaviour is amplifying who you are or replacing it.

Most importantly, you can reclaim your right to exist beyond the scroll, to experience moments that don't need to be shared, to live memories that don't need to be archived. You can begin to cultivate a self that is whole even when no one is watching.

Because while your digital ghost may live forever in data, your actual self, the one that breathes, senses, questions, and changes, is here, now, and deserving of your full attention.

27

Chapter 8: Algorithmic Life

You might believe that the choices you make online are your own. The videos you watch, the people you follow, the music you discover, and the news you read all emerge from personal taste and free decision. But in truth, the vast majority of what you see, click, and consume on your devices is not chosen by you at all. It's selected for you. And often, it's determined by algorithms that understand your behaviour better than you do.

At first, it feels convenient. Your streaming service suggests a movie right when you're too tired to decide. A playlist shows up on a stressful day and somehow fits your mood. An ad appears for something you didn't even realize you wanted yet. These aren't accidents. They are outcomes of predictive modelling based on your data, what you've clicked on, hovered over, scrolled past, or lingered on in the past. Every interaction, no matter how small, is recorded and used to shape what you'll see next.

Over time, these systems begin to sculpt the world you live in, subtly but powerfully. Your social feeds narrow to align with your existing views. Your recommendations reflect more of what you've already liked. Your preferences are nudged, reinforced, and looped back to you in an ever-tightening circle. You are no longer merely navigating the internet; you are being navigated through it.

This is the architecture of the algorithmic life: a world filtered, personalized, and optimized for engagement, but not necessarily for growth, complexity, or truth. It offers comfort over challenge, predictability over discovery. And because the changes happen gradually, invisibly, you don't notice how the edges of your perspective are shrinking.

This personalization isn't just about content; it begins to shape identity. What you're shown becomes part of how you define yourself. The articles you read, the influencers you follow, and the trends you absorb all contribute to a sense of who you are and what matters. But if these inputs are subtly manipulated to keep you engaged, then your identity is being shaped not by your values, but by engineered design.

The deeper cost of this system is choice. You believe you're choosing, but your options are limited to what the algorithm offers. You are presented with a curated menu and asked to select from it repeatedly, reinforcing patterns that are profitable for the platform but narrowing for you. The illusion of freedom becomes a trap: you scroll endlessly, but within invisible walls.

Even your curiosity can become domesticated. You stop looking for what isn't served to you. You grow used to convenience, to passively consuming what's presented rather than actively seeking what's not. The frictionless ease of being fed replaces the richness of exploration.

To live an algorithmic life is to live inside a feedback loop. And feedback loops, by their nature, favour repetition over evolution.

Yet this isn't inevitable. The tools that shape your digital experience are powerful, but not absolute. You can begin to notice what you're being shown, and what you're not. You can step outside your usual feeds, seek sources that challenge rather than confirm, and spend time in spaces not designed to manipulate your behaviour.

It starts with small acts of digital resistance. Choosing not to click the first suggestion. Searching for what you want instead of settling for what's offered. Following creators and thinkers who don't fit neatly into your algorithmic bubble. Reading things slowly, deeply, and all the way through.

Reclaiming your digital choices means accepting some friction. It's easier to go with the flow of what's pushed your way. But ease is not the same as autonomy. And comfort is not the same as truth.

The algorithm isn't evil. It's efficient. But what it optimizes for is engagement, not understanding, profit, not freedom. If you want to live a whole digital life, one grounded in awareness, agency, and depth, you'll have to move beyond what the system wants you to see.

You are not a passive consumer of content. You are a participant in the shaping of your mind.

And that begins by choosing not just what to click, but what to seek.

Chapter 9: Cognitive Overwhelm, 24/7

There's a particular kind of tired that doesn't come from physical exertion. It's not the ache after a long walk or the drowsiness after a poor night's sleep. It's a quieter, more elusive fatigue, the kind that settles into your mind like fog. You might not even notice it at first. There's no single moment when it begins. But gradually, you realize that concentrating feels harder, that simple decisions start to feel heavier, that your thoughts scatter more easily than they used to.

This is cognitive overwhelm, and it is increasingly becoming the default mental state for people living in a world designed for nonstop stimulation.

It's easy to mistake it for laziness or personal failure. After all, how can someone feel mentally worn out when they've done nothing "hard" all day? But this confusion stems from a misunderstanding of what effort looks like in the digital age. Mental fatigue doesn't always come from solving complex problems. It often comes from managing too many small things, too often, with too little space in between.

Every time you check your phone, your brain is forced to shift gears. You scan a message, remember a task, respond to a notification, glance at a headline, and look at an image. Each of these micro-interactions demands a little attention, a little memory, a little processing. On their own, they seem insignificant. But when they accumulate across hundreds of moments throughout the day, the load becomes staggering.

It's not just the quantity of inputs; it's the fragmentation. When your attention is constantly interrupted, your brain never enters the deeper states of focus that allow for clarity and integration. Your thoughts remain scattered, your awareness thinly spread. It's like trying to read a novel while someone taps your shoulder every thirty seconds. Even if the interruptions are minor, their impact is cumulative.

And these inputs don't stop. Long after work hours end, long after your body has settled into rest, the mental loops continue. Do you remember that comment you never replied to? You replay a conversation from earlier. You scroll a little more before sleep.

Even in bed, the glow of the screen follows you. What you consume lingers, whether or not you want it to.

Cognitive overwhelm isn't just about information volume. It's about emotional load. Much of what you encounter online is charged with urgency, outrage, or subtle comparison. News alerts, social updates, performance metrics, and algorithmic nudges all ask for something from you. They want your reaction, your approval, your participation. They invite you to weigh in, measure up, and take sides.

Your brain, meanwhile, is left trying to keep up, evaluating, responding, absorbing, even when no action is required. Over time, this hyper-responsiveness blurs the boundary between what matters and what demands attention. Your nervous system doesn't distinguish between a life-altering message and a trivial ping. It simply registers input and keeps you alert.

This is how you can feel exhausted at the end of a day without being able to point to anything substantial you accomplished. Your mind has been in motion, but never at rest. Your attention has been consumed, but rarely nourished.

The worst part is that this state starts to feel normal. You begin to expect your brain to feel foggy, distracted, and overstimulated. You adapt your life to accommodate the clutter: shorter reading sessions, lighter conversations, less time spent in silence. But adaptation is not the same as wellness. Just because you can function doesn't mean you're thriving.

So what's the alternative?

The first step is recognition. Acknowledge that cognitive overload isn't just a side effect of modern life; it's a signal that your mind is operating beyond its intended capacity. Your attention is a finite resource. When you treat it like something infinite, you burn out not just your focus, but your ability to live with clarity and intention.

The next step is simplification. Start by reducing the number of channels competing for your mental bandwidth. This might mean fewer tabs open. Fewer notifications are turned on—more intentional gaps in your day when no new information is allowed in. You can create small sanctuaries of silence where your brain is free to reset.

Recovery from cognitive overwhelm doesn't require dramatic withdrawal. It requires consistency. It means choosing slowness where you can—protecting mental whitespace and reclaiming the capacity to think one complete thought at a time.

Because the goal isn't just to clear your mind, it's to inhabit it again.

Chapter 10: When Devices Parent Us

There was a time, not long ago, when boredom was a standard part of childhood. Waiting in a grocery store line, sitting in the back seat during errands, enduring long family dinners, these were moments when a child had little to do but observe, fidget, imagine, or daydream. These pauses, as dull as they sometimes felt, were essential terrain for emotional development. In boredom, a child encountered themselves. They learned how to self-soothe, how to invent games from nothing, how to sit with discomfort without needing it resolved for them.

Today, those spaces are disappearing.

Watch a toddler in a stroller at a restaurant. Or a child at the doctor's office. A teenager at the table with their family. Increasingly, a screen is placed in their hands, sometimes out of necessity, sometimes habit, sometimes desperation. The reason is always understandable. The world is chaotic. Parents are overwhelmed. The child is melting down, and the screen calms them almost instantly. A few taps on a screen can soothe, distract, and entertain. It works. But over time, that convenience begins to come at a cost.

What we are seeing, in real time, is a shift in how children learn to regulate their attention and their emotions. Where once those skills were cultivated slowly, through human interaction, solitude, or play, they are now being outsourced to digital tools. The tablet becomes the pacifier. The phone becomes the babysitter. The algorithm becomes the co-parent.

This isn't a critique of parenting; it's a reflection on culture. The demands placed on modern families are relentless. Dual-income households, unpredictable schedules, and shrinking support networks; it's no wonder that screens become lifelines. But the devices we hand to our children don't just fill the moment; they shape the mind.

When a child turns to a device to soothe every moment of restlessness, they miss out on building the internal muscles of regulation. They become accustomed to stimulation as a solution. Quiet becomes unbearable. Stillness is interpreted as a void. Emotional discomfort is met not with conversation or reflection but with animation, games, and scrolls. This doesn't teach resilience; it bypasses it.

But the impact isn't only on children. Adults are not exempt from this new dynamic. Many of us grew up before smartphones, but we've absorbed the same habits. We reach for our phones at the slightest twinge of discomfort. In waiting rooms, we no longer make eye contact with strangers or sit quietly with our thoughts. In difficult emotional moments, instead of pausing or turning inward, we turn outward, to the screen, the feed, the flickering distraction. In doing so, we unintentionally model the same behaviour for the next generation.

This is how devices become not just tools but caregivers. They mediate our discomfort. They become the first line of response to distress, fatigue, awkwardness, or boredom. And because they're always available, always responsive, they start to replace older, slower forms of self-regulation. We stop practicing presence because presence no longer feels necessary.

But what's lost in the process is hard to quantify. It's the quiet resilience of a child who learns how to entertain themselves with imagination. It's the depth of a conversation that happens because there was nothing else to do. It's the joy of attention that stays in one place long enough to notice something small and meaningful.

There's no simple fix. No parent wants to be scolded for surviving the day. No adult needs another lecture about screen time. What's needed is awareness and grace. To recognize that the device is fulfilling a role it was never intended for. That it's too much power, handed too early, without enough guidance. And to begin, gently, to take some of that power back.

It might look like leaving the tablet at home for certain outings, even if it means a child complains. It might look like letting boredom stretch a little longer without rescuing it. It might look like choosing a few screen-free rituals in the day: a shared meal, a walk, bedtime stories. These choices don't have to be rigid or perfect. They only have to be consistent.

For adults, the shift starts with honesty. Recognizing when the phone has become an emotional crutch. Admitting when the scroll is about escape. And slowly, replacing that reflex with something slower, something less immediately gratifying, but more nourishing.

Because attention is not something we can teach by telling. It's something we pass on by how we live. If we want our children to know how to be present in their lives, we have to show them what that looks like, even when it's messy, even when it's imperfect.

Especially then.

Part II: The Hidden Architecture

Chapter 11: This Wasn't an Accident

If it feels like your phone has an uncanny ability to pull you in, it's not your imagination. If you've ever found yourself opening an app without realizing it, or losing thirty minutes to a feed you only meant to glance at, you're not alone, and you're not failing. What you're experiencing is the result of careful, deliberate design. This isn't a case of clumsy engineering that accidentally made us compulsive users. This was the plan.

The phrase "attention economy" gets thrown around often, but few pause to consider what it means. In simple terms, your attention, what you look at, how long you look, what you click on, what you return to, is one of the most valuable commodities in the world today. Tech companies don't sell you their products. You are the product. Or more precisely, your attention is.

This shift didn't happen overnight. In the early days of the internet, monetization came through traditional routes: banner ads, pay-per-click campaigns, and basic display advertising. But soon, companies realized that the more time users spent on their platforms, the more ads could be shown, the more data could be harvested, and the more behaviour could be predicted and influenced. Time spent wasn't just a metric. It was the currency of control.

To capture more of your time, engineers and designers began applying behavioural science principles in ways that were once reserved for slot machines and casino floors. Variable reward schedules, infinite content loops, and frictionless interfaces were introduced not to enhance your life, but to increase your engagement.

What emerged from this was not a neutral technology, but a psychological architecture. Your device is now an environment shaped by people you'll never meet, people whose goals may be very different from yours.

For example, that simple act of scrolling down a feed, which feels like a natural gesture, is a carefully chosen mechanism.

Before infinite scroll, web pages had endings. You would reach the bottom, pause, and decide whether to continue. That break offered you a moment of agency. But the infinite scroll removed that pause. The page never ends. And when there is no ending, there is no decision to stop. That absence of stopping points keeps your brain suspended in motion.

Notifications, too, have been redesigned over time. Once, they were functional, with alerts for messages or missed calls. Now they're emotional. They appear in bright colours. They tap into social instincts. They promise recognition or reward. That little red badge doesn't just tell you something has happened; it tells you it might matter. And the uncertainty is what hooks you.

Even the way your phone vibrates is engineered. Haptic feedback is tuned to feel like a physical nudge, not a mechanical buzz. It's subtle, intimate, like someone tapping your shoulder. It doesn't just get your attention. It makes the device feel alive, attentive to you, pulling you in with every gesture.

And then there's the data. Every click, every search, every scroll is recorded, not only to improve your personal experience, as the marketing language claims, but to refine the systems that predict your behaviour. These systems learn what holds your attention, what outrages you, what soothes you, and what makes you feel connected or excluded. Then they deliver more of it. Not to inform you, but to engage you. Not to broaden your mind, but to deepen your dependence.

The result is that your digital environment is no longer passive. It's persuasive. It guides your decisions without forcing them. It nudges, it suggests, it frames. And over time, those micro-influences accumulate into habits, many of which feel like your own choices, even though they've been shaped upstream by design.

This isn't to say a villain is twirling a mustache behind the screen. Most of the people designing these systems didn't set out to manipulate or addict. Many believed they were building tools for connection, productivity, and creativity. And in some ways, they did. But when a business model depends on capturing and monetizing your attention, every design decision becomes a choice between what's good for you and what's good for the platform's bottom line.

And in that equation, your well-being often takes a backseat.

The implications go beyond personal distraction. When millions of people live inside systems that constantly hijack attention, you begin to see the societal impact: fractured focus, rising anxiety, cultural polarization, shortened tempers. What looks like personal tech use adds up to a collective crisis of attention.

But this chapter isn't about despair. It's about clarity. Understanding that the forces shaping your attention are intentional, not accidental, gives you back some power. You're not wrestling with vague distractions. You're navigating systems designed to keep you engaged. And when you see those systems clearly, you can begin to resist them with intention.

In the chapters that follow, we'll dig deeper into the specific mechanisms behind this persuasive design, how your brain is being trained, what reward loops keep you returning, and what you can do to interrupt the cycle, because awareness is not enough. You need new patterns, new boundaries, and new ways of relating to your tools.

But before that work begins, you must hold this truth close: the erosion of your focus was not your failure.

This was not an accident.

Chapter 12: Hooked by Design

There is a reason you feel the pull. That familiar itch in your hand when your phone isn't nearby. That flicker of impatience during a quiet moment, resolved only by a scroll. The almost unconscious way your thumb moves across a screen, even before you've decided what you're looking for. These aren't random habits. They're learned responses, carefully crafted, thoroughly tested, and widely deployed across the digital landscape. You are hooked, but not by accident. You were designed to be.

Much of what governs our current digital behaviour can be traced back to a now-iconic model known as the "Hooked Cycle." Coined by behavioural designer Nir Eyal, it was initially proposed to help tech entrepreneurs build habit-forming products. But what began as a business framework has since become a blueprint for shaping behaviour on a global scale.

The Hooked model consists of four simple stages: trigger, action, reward, and investment. It starts with a trigger, something that initiates behaviour. This might be external, like a notification or banner. But the most potent triggers are internal: boredom, loneliness, and anxiety. These emotional discomforts don't arrive with a ding or flash. They creep in quietly and send you reaching for the device.

Then comes the action, the behaviour that follows the trigger. Usually, something simple: opening an app, refreshing a feed, tapping into a story. In most cases, the action is done without conscious deliberation. The easier it is to perform, the more likely you are to repeat it.

The third step is where things get sticky: the variable reward. Instead of offering the same outcome every time, platforms introduce a kind of lottery mechanism. Sometimes the feed is dull. Sometimes it's thrilling. Sometimes there's a message. Sometimes nothing at all. The unpredictability mimics the psychology of gambling, keeping you engaged precisely because you don't know what's coming next.

Finally, the investment phase: the idea that the more you interact with a platform —commenting, liking, posting, and building a history —the more invested you become. Your time, attention, and social energy start to live inside the app. You've made a kind of digital down payment, and walking away becomes harder because of what you've already given.

This cycle repeats itself hundreds of times a day. And because it maps directly onto the structure of your brain's reward system, it becomes internalized. You begin to self-trigger. You no longer need a notification to check your phone. Your brain has learned the rhythm. Emotional discomfort becomes a cue to seek relief through digital engagement.

What's most concerning is how little effort is required on your part for the loop to continue. The system does the heavy lifting. It monitors your behaviour, learns your triggers, and refines the reward schedules. Your only role is to respond, again and again, until the behaviour feels less like a choice and more like a reflex.

And it works. It works because it doesn't rely on logic. It bypasses rational thinking and taps into older, more automatic parts of the mind. You don't scroll Instagram because you believe it will improve your life. You scroll because the pattern is already running.

This isn't a flaw in your personality. It's a feature of your biology. The human brain is remarkably responsive to repetition and reward. What's new is the scale and precision of these systems. For the first time in history, behaviour design has access to billions of data points per day, refined by machine learning, targeted to each individual's tendencies and vulnerabilities.

Some argue that this makes the platforms addictive. Others say "addiction" is too strong, that what we're seeing is just deep engagement. But whatever term we use, the effect is the same: a world in which people are no longer choosing when and how to use technology. They are being selected.

It would be easy to place blame entirely on the designers, to cast the entire industry as manipulative or malicious. But the truth is more complex. Many of the systems now causing harm were built with good intentions. They were designed to be helpful, efficient, even delightful. And for a while, they were. But over time, the incentives shifted. The goal shifted from helping users live well to keeping them coming back.

In this shift, something essential was lost: the understanding that attention is sacred. That human behaviour is not a game to be hacked. Those tools should serve, not consume.

So what now?

You can't unbuild the Hooked Cycle. But you can unhook yourself from it. You can learn to recognize the loop when it begins. You can slow the trigger. Interrupt the action. Question the reward. Withdraw the investment. These aren't one-time decisions. They are small, repeated acts of attention, each one reclaiming a bit more space between you and the design.

And as you reclaim that space, something begins to shift. You start to feel the difference between compulsion and intention. You remember what it's like to use a tool, rather than be used by it. You rediscover the possibility of being present, entirely, quietly, without needing a reward to make it worthwhile.

Because once you see the hook, you can choose not to bite.

Chapter 13: Social Validation as Currency

You post a photo. A few moments later, a heart appears. Then another. A comment pops up: "You look amazing." Someone shares it. The feedback loop begins. You feel a little lift in your chest, a flicker of warmth, the sense that you've been seen. It doesn't feel like a transaction, but it is. And you're not trading information, time, or even content. You're trading in something much older and more instinctive: social validation.

This is the invisible currency of the digital world, the attention, approval, and affirmation we offer and seek, one click at a time. On the surface, it looks like a harmless interaction. I like it here. A thumbs up there. A comment, a share. But underneath, these tiny exchanges tap into a part of the human brain that has always been wired to care about social standing.

In evolutionary terms, belonging wasn't optional; it was survival. Being part of a group meant protection, resources, and continuity. Rejection meant risk. Our brains evolved to be exquisitely attuned to cues of acceptance and exclusion. Today, that same neural machinery lights up in response to digital signals, likes, comments, tags, and mentions. A glowing red heart triggers the same chemical pathways that, millennia ago, might have been activated by a nod around a campfire.

But what once happened slowly, over time, in the context of authentic relationships, now happens rapidly, continuously, in front of a crowd. The metrics are visible. Quantified. Comparable. You don't just know you're liked, you can count it. You don't just feel included; you can measure it against someone else.

And the platforms are built to reward you for caring.

The more validation you receive, the more your content is shown. The more engagement you inspire, the more visible you become. The system is self-reinforcing: approval breeds exposure, and exposure creates more opportunity for approval. Whether you're aware of it or not, this system begins to influence what you post, how you present yourself, and which aspects of your personality you prioritize.

Over time, your identity subtly orients itself toward what is most likely to be rewarded.

This doesn't make you shallow. It makes you human.

But the danger lies in the distortion. When social approval becomes the primary measure of value, your sense of self begins to externalize. Instead of asking, "Does this reflect who I am?" you begin to ask, "Will this be liked?" The desire to be seen becomes entangled with the fear of being invisible. You may start to curate your life for its reaction, rather than for its meaning.

This currency also changes the way you relate to others. Every post becomes a performance. Every comment is a signal. Every absence is a silence to be interpreted. Instead of connecting deeply, you begin to monitor and compare. Their likes versus yours. Their moments versus yours. Their audience, their relevance, and their rising visibility all start to matter more than they should.

Even joy becomes filtered through the lens of shareability. The experience isn't complete until it's validated. But this cycle leaves something behind: the quiet, private satisfaction of a life lived for its own sake.

When validation becomes currency, authenticity becomes collateral, not in every case, and not immediately. But gradually, subtly, you begin to feel less free to express without an audience, less willing to exist without proof. And the craving is endless because the system was built to keep you hungry.

You can sense it, can't you? That slight disappointment when a post doesn't land. The twinge when someone else goes viral. The habitual return to your profile, to see how it's performing. These aren't failures of character. There are signs that your nervous system has adapted to an economy you didn't consciously choose.

But you can opt out of the terms, even if you stay in the system.

You can begin by noticing. The next time you post, ask yourself why. What are you hoping to receive? What would it mean to post it and walk away? What would it feel like to live a moment that no one else witnessed, and to let it remain yours?

You can make room for validation from fewer, more trustworthy sources. Choose to share less broadly, more intentionally. Nurture conversations that go below the surface. Shift your attention from the number of responses to the depth of connection—trade applause for resonance.

And perhaps most importantly, re-learn the feeling of doing something well without showing it. Let a day be meaningful even if it's undocumented. Let your identity be shaped in the absence of eyes.

Social validation is not wrong. It's woven into who we are. But when it becomes the only signal we trust, we begin to lose touch with quieter forms of knowing, intuition, memory, and meaning. And those, too, deserve your attention.

Because your worth was never meant to be measured in hearts and counts.

Chapter 14: When Notifications Became Dopamine

You're in the middle of something, maybe reading, maybe cooking, maybe having a conversation, and then you hear it. A buzz, a chime, a banner sliding across the top of your screen. A notification. Something has happened. Someone has reached out. You don't know what it is yet, but you feel a small charge, a flicker of curiosity—your attention shifts. Even if you don't look right away, your mind does. And if you do look, you're rewarded. Or not. Either way, the loop is complete.

It might seem like a small thing, one notification, one quick check. But that single moment is part of a much larger system, one that runs not just on convenience but on chemistry. Your brain is being trained, at a neurobiological level, to respond to these cues in the same way it might react to a potential reward, a social signal, or a survival threat. And the training is relentless.

The story begins with dopamine. Often misunderstood as the "pleasure chemical," dopamine isn't about feeling good. It's about wanting. It's what drives you to seek, to pursue, to anticipate. When something potentially rewarding is on the horizon, your brain releases dopamine, sharpening your focus, increasing motivation, and locking in attention. This mechanism evolved to help you survive, find food, pursue relationships, and navigate complex environments. But today, it's being triggered by pings.

Notifications are designed to tap into this seeking system. They are not neutral alerts. They are carefully crafted signals meant to interrupt, to invite, to tempt. The colour red is often chosen deliberately; your brain is wired to respond to red as urgent. The sound design is tuned to be just noticeable enough to trigger curiosity without being immediately dismissible. Even the timing is calculated. Some platforms batch notifications so that you get them when you're more likely to act on them. Others use random delivery to keep you checking, just in case.

Every time you check and find something new, your brain gets a hit of dopamine. That hit reinforces the behaviour. You learn, subconsciously, that checking brings reward, or at least the chance of one. And because the reward is unpredictable, the checking becomes compulsive. This is the essence of a variable reward loop: a behaviour repeated in anticipation of a payoff that sometimes arrives and sometimes doesn't.

It's the exact mechanism that keeps people pulling slot machine handles.

But unlike slot machines, your phone is always with you. The loop doesn't require a visit to a casino. It runs quietly in your pocket, at your desk, beside your bed. Over time, this loop doesn't just train your behaviour; it rewires your baseline. You start to feel agitated in silence. You reach for your phone without realizing it. You find yourself craving input, not because something is wrong, but because your brain has been conditioned to expect it.

And the deeper cost isn't just time, it's attention fragmentation. When your focus is continually interrupted, your brain loses the ability to sustain deep concentration. You begin to live in a state of partial focus, always ready to shift, never fully arriving. It becomes harder to read, to listen, to be still. The rhythm of your device hijacks your cognitive rhythm.

This isn't a failure of willpower. It's a predictable outcome of design intersecting with biology.

When notifications became dopamine, the game changed.

The effects ripple outward. In your work, where do you find it harder to enter a flow? In your relationships, where eye contact is more often with screens than faces. In your rest, which is disturbed not just by the light of your phone, but by the mental residue of alerts that still echo in your nervous system long after you've seen them.

But here's the hopeful part: just as this loop was learned, it can be unlearned.

You can begin by noticing your patterns. How often do you check your phone when there's no notification at all? What emotions precede those checks? What does your body feel like right before you reach for it? These are clues. The more aware you become of the triggers, the more space you create to make a different choice.

Then, you can take steps to reduce the grip of the loop. Turn off non-essential notifications. Move tempting apps off your home screen. Create specific windows of time when your phone is in another room, or better yet, powered down. These aren't acts of deprivation. They are acts of restoration. You're not punishing yourself. You're giving your nervous system a break.

And over time, something begins to return: your baseline. That quieter hum of thought. That deeper quality of focus. That moment where you're fully inside an activity, unfragmented.

Because while your brain has been shaped by technology, it can be reshaped by intention.

Notifications will continue to exist. Some will still be useful. But they no longer have to own your attention. You can move from reactivity to choice. From craving to presence and from compulsive checking to spacious living.

And in that space, something precious returns: your sovereignty over your mind.

Chapter 15: Digital Addictions Without Shame

When you hear the word addiction, your mind probably conjures something extreme, a crisis, an unravelling, something that derails a life. But addiction doesn't always roar. Sometimes, it hums quietly under the surface of your day. You feel it not as a catastrophe, but as a compulsion. As the subtle inability to stop, even when part of you wants to.

This is where many people find themselves with technology. Not destroyed by it, but tethered. Not overtaken, but quietly owned.

You check your phone the moment you wake up, not because you need to, but because it feels unnatural not to. You scroll through feeds with a glazed-over mind, not even enjoying them, just… continuing. You promise yourself one more video, one more update, one more message. Then you do it again. You're not in crisis. You're just not in control.

And yet, when you try to name this relationship, when you speak the word addiction, it often comes with shame as if the problem is a personal defect. A weakness of will. A lack of discipline. You look at others who seem to handle it better and quietly wonder what's wrong with you.

But the truth is, you've been living in an environment engineered for dependence.

Digital addiction is not a character flaw. It is a consequence of long-term, high-frequency exposure to systems that are optimized to exploit the vulnerabilities of your attention, your curiosity, your need to connect, and your fear of missing out.

And it happens gradually, not through a single moment of surrender, but through thousands of tiny interactions. Each swipe, each ping, each dopamine hit etches a groove into your habits. One day, you realize you no longer reach for your phone; you have it in your hand. It's already there.

Unlike chemical addictions, digital addictions are socially accepted, even rewarded. No one judges you for being reachable, responsive, and up-to-date. They expect it. The tools that hook you are also the ones that make you efficient, connected, and visible. This makes the addiction harder to name, let alone resist.

The same platforms that exhaust you are also where your community lives, where your job communicates, and where your memories are stored. Quitting entirely feels impossible. And so, the cycle continues, not with urgency, but with quiet resignation.

But naming something is the first act of liberation.

You are not the problem. You are a person living in an attention economy that profits from your compulsions. You are responding, often predictably, to the most persuasive technologies ever built. These tools were not made to be neutral. They were made to be sticky. Your behaviour is not a failure; it's a mirror reflecting the success of their design.

So instead of shame, try compassion.

Notice when you feel powerless, not as a sign of weakness, but as an invitation. What are you seeking when you reach for the screen? What emotion lives beneath the habit? Boredom? Anxiety? Loneliness? Fatigue? So often, our compulsive behaviours are not about the content but about the feelings we are trying to soothe or escape.

This is where real change begins, not with blame, but with curiosity.

Ask: When do I feel most drawn to this? When do I think most clearheaded and alive? What patterns am I living inside? And are they mine?

Because here's the truth: addiction thrives in silence. In secrecy. In the space where shame keeps you from asking better questions. The moment you begin to observe your habits without judgment, you create the possibility for choice. Not all at once. Not in some grand gesture. But one breath at a time.

You can begin by experimenting gently. Leave your phone in another room during meals. Notice what comes up. Try walking without headphones. See what thoughts surface. Remove a social media app for a weekend. Notice if the world feels emptier, or if your mind begins to settle. These aren't detoxes. They're not punishment. They are reconnections with your agency, your presence, and your life as it unfolds without digital mediation.

And when you relapse, and you will, that's not failure either. It's part of the pattern. The point is not to eliminate every reflex, but to stop living in default mode. To remember, again and again, that you are more than your behaviours. You are the one observing them.

There is no need to villainize technology or yourself. There is only the invitation to live awake, to meet your tools with awareness, to let go of what's hollow, to build new habits from a place of clarity, not shame.

Because addiction without shame opens the door to healing.

And that door is still open, no matter how long you've been hooked.

Chapter 16: The Economics of Your Attention

Most people don't think of themselves as part of an economy. You work, you earn, you spend; that part is clear. But outside of those visible transactions, another kind of market exists. One where the currency isn't dollars, crypto, or gold. It's your attention.

Your time, your gaze, your clicks, your curiosity, these are among the most valuable assets in the modern world. Not because of what they are in isolation, but because of what they enable. Wherever your attention goes, your decisions follow. And wherever your choices go, your data, money, and energy tend to go, too.

Attention has always been a form of power. In past centuries, it was the domain of orators, politicians, artists, and religious leaders. Those who could gather and direct attention could shape minds, beliefs, and behaviour. But in the digital age, attention has become something else entirely: a resource that can be harvested, measured, monetized, and traded, at scale.

This shift didn't happen by accident. As traditional advertising lost its grip in print and broadcast media, tech platforms realized that what they offered wasn't just access to users, it was access to users' minds. And the more time they could capture, the more valuable their platforms became.

Every platform you use for "free" is not free. The price you pay is subtle but constant. It's paid in moments of distraction. In fractured thought. In decisions influenced by nudges, you didn't notice. It's spent in the cumulative cost of thousands of interruptions you didn't consciously choose.

Think about the structure of these platforms. They are not designed to inform, entertain, or connect you out of altruism. Those may be the outcomes, but the design is optimized for one goal: engagement. Every second you linger, every scroll you complete, every loop you rewatch, increases the likelihood that you'll stay longer and see more ads.

The more predictable your behaviour becomes, the easier it is to sell access to you. Not just your identity, but your patterns. Your preferences. Your susceptibilities. What outrages you?

What soothes you? What keeps you up at night, and what makes you click without thinking? This is the data that fuels the engine.

You are not the customer. You are the inventory.

And yet, the platforms don't feel extractive. They feel personal. Tailored. Friendly. The algorithm seems to know you. But it doesn't know you in the human sense; it knows your behaviour. And the goal isn't to make you wise, or fulfilled, or free. The goal is to keep you watching.

What makes this system especially potent is that it often works beneath the threshold of awareness. Most people don't wake up and think, "Today I'm going to give my mind away to a handful of apps." They check in, here and there. They reply to messages. They glance at the news. But these small acts accumulate. And each one trains the brain to expect more of the same.

The economy of attention doesn't require you to believe in it. It only requires you to participate.

This might sound bleak. But understanding the mechanics of this economy is the first step toward reclaiming your place in it, not as a product, but as a person.

You begin by asking different questions. Not, "Is this app good or bad?" but "What is this platform asking of my mind?" Not, "Do I like using it?" but "Who benefits when I spend time here?" And not, "Is this content interesting?" but "Is it worth the cost of my attention?"

Because make no mistake, there is always a cost. Every moment you spend consuming something is a moment you didn't spend creating, reflecting, resting, or connecting with someone in front of you. Time is finite. Energy is limited. And attention, once paid, can't be retrieved.

This isn't about guilt. It's about discernment.

You can begin to view your attention as a resource to be invested wisely, not hoarded, not drained, but directed. Just as you wouldn't give your money to any stranger on the street who asks for it, you don't need to provide your attention to every notification, post, or trending topic.

Ask: Is this building something in me? Is this deepening my understanding? Is this aligning with who I want to be?

When you start asking those questions, the terrain changes, you notice what pulls at you, and what holds you. You begin to set boundaries, not out of deprivation, but from a place of value. You realize that your attention is not just what you give away. It's what you live inside.

And as with any economy, there is power in choosing how to participate.

Because you are not just a passive node in a system. You are a sovereign mind. And your attention, once reclaimed, can become the most liberating force in your life.

Chapter 17: Surveillance Disguised as Convenience

It begins with small permissions. A map app wants to access your location "only while using." A calendar asks to sync with your contacts. A weather app requests background updates. A note-taking app wants microphone access, for dictation, it says. You grant them. Not because you've read the terms, but because it's faster to agree than to pause. Besides, you trust the trade-off. You're getting something worthwhile. Directions. Simpler logins. A personalized feed. Convenience.

But over time, the permission becomes the platform.

Each of these moments — the tap to allow, the check of a box, the default setting left untouched — accumulates into a system. And that system does more than serve you. It watches you. Learns you. Not in a malicious, movie-villain way, but in a patient, persistent one. Like a quiet observer taking notes on everything, you do: where you go, who you message, what you search, when you scroll, how long you linger.

You've been told it's anonymous. Aggregated. Harmless. Maybe you believe that. Perhaps it doesn't bother you. But the reality is that we are living in the most surveilled era in human history, and most of us handed over the keys with a smile.

Surveillance used to mean someone watching from the shadows. Now it means algorithms listening to your pocket. Every device you carry is a sensor. Every click is a signal. And nearly every service you use, especially if it's free, is funded not by your subscription, but by your data.

And yet, it rarely feels intrusive. That's the brilliance of the design. The tracking isn't cloaked in threat; it's wrapped in helpfulness. Want reminders based on your location? Let us follow you. Want smarter ads? Let us read your messages. Want to autofill your passwords, your preferences, your life? Let us know who you are.

The pitch is always easy. And it's not a lie, life is easier when everything is integrated. When your preferences are remembered, your routes are predicted, your habits anticipated. You forgot your coffee shop order, but your phone hasn't. You didn't write down the appointment, but your assistant, virtual, ever-present, has you covered.

And that's the trade we've made: information for convenience. But convenience isn't neutral. It's curated. It shapes how you move, what you see, and who you talk to. It reduces friction, yes, but it also reduces autonomy.

Because when your preferences are predicted, you stop choosing. When your options are filtered, you stop wondering. And when your behaviour is tracked, scored, and fed back to you, you begin to internalize the logic of the system. You start thinking in the language of algorithms: what's efficient, what's trending, what's optimized.

But optimized for whom?

That's the question we rarely stop to ask. Who benefits from your constant visibility? Who profits when you trade privacy for personalization?

The answer isn't just advertisers; it's the entire infrastructure of the attention economy. The more predictable you are, the more valuable you become. And predictability requires data. So, the system rewards oversharing, incentivizes tracking, and makes it increasingly difficult to opt out. Try to turn off tracking completely, and you'll often be met with warnings: this app may not work as intended. This feature will be limited. You'll lose your personalized experience.

And somewhere along the way, you begin to accept that full participation requires full exposure.

But it doesn't.

You are allowed to draw a line. To ask: what am I giving up for this ease? What does it cost to be constantly known? Not just by friends, but by machines?

The answer is subtle, but profound: it costs sovereignty. The space to be unknown, even to yourself. The freedom to be inconsistent, messy, and private. To have parts of your life that are not optimized, categorized, or sold.

Reclaiming that space doesn't require moving to the woods or smashing your phone. It begins with awareness. You can start by reviewing your app permissions, not just once, but regularly.

You can turn off location tracking where it's unnecessary. Choose browsers and tools that prioritize privacy. Support services that charge a fee instead of harvesting your behaviour. Slow down when something asks for access.

Most of all, you can challenge the story that ease is always worth the price.

Because the truth is, what's marketed as convenience is often just control, disguised in a user-friendly interface.

And if you're not paying attention, you won't even notice that you've traded your privacy for a slightly faster load time.

But once you do notice, you start to see the choice.

Not between tech and no tech, but between passive acceptance and conscious participation.

Not between visibility and invisibility, but between being watched and being seen on your terms.

Not between convenience and chaos, but between ease that serves you and ease that sells you.

The difference matters.

Chapter 18: The Performance Self

There's a version of you that lives online. You curate it, even if you don't mean to. It's built from pictures, words, likes, affiliations, things you share, and things you don't. Sometimes, this version feels aligned with who you are. Other times, it feels like a costume that no longer fits, but you keep wearing it because everyone else still thinks it's you.

This is the performance self.

In the offline world, identity is fluid. You show different sides of yourself depending on where you are and who you're with. The way you speak to a friend over coffee is different from how you present in a meeting. But those versions come and go. They're grounded in physical time, embodied presence. They change.

Online, the self becomes stickier.

You post something clever. People respond. It's liked, shared, remembered. That response feels good. It reinforces the part of you that made the post. So maybe you do it again. Not because it's forced, but because it works. You're building something. A personal brand, perhaps, or just a version of you that feels consistent and liked. But slowly, subtly, you start performing that version more often. You stay within the tone that garners approval. You highlight the traits people recognize. You begin to edit.

This is not vanity. It's instinct. Social animals adapt to social rewards. We're wired for mirroring, belonging, and validation. The problem isn't the performance; it's when we forget it's a performance. When the feedback we receive begins to shape not just what we do, but how we see ourselves.

You stop writing what you feel and start writing what will resonate. You stop exploring new interests because they don't "fit" your profile. You hesitate before posting something vulnerable because it might confuse the audience you've trained to expect something else. You begin to live within the lines you've drawn for yourself, and the platform keeps handing you the brush.

It happens everywhere, not just on social media, but in inboxes, profile bios, and comment threads. The self becomes visible, and the visible self must be managed. You are aware of the eyes. Not one set of eyes, but thousands, ambient, imagined. You perform for them, and eventually, you may not remember how to be offstage.

For younger generations, there may never have been a time before this. Adolescents now grow up not just under peer scrutiny, but platform scrutiny. Every post, every photo, every message is archived in some form. Mistakes are less forgettable. Reinvention is harder. The pressure to be polished is not developmental; it's digital. And with that pressure comes anxiety, perfectionism, and an unrelenting awareness of the audience.

But this isn't just a generational issue. Adults feel it too. The pressure to be "on," to cultivate a professional persona, a lifestyle aesthetic, an ideological alignment. To say the right things. To be palatable. Even in private spaces, we carry the residue of performance. We think in captions. We narrate our lives as if someone is watching.

Because in many ways, someone always is.

The platforms don't just hold your content. They shape it. Their design encourages repetition. If a post performs well, you're more likely to be shown. If you stay consistent, you're rewarded. Deviate, and you risk losing traction. This creates a subtle pressure toward sameness, not just within your profile, but across the culture.

The result is that the self-perceived performance becomes safer than the actual one. It's polished, pre-approved, algorithmically advantaged. And yet, it leaves something behind: the freedom to be unfinished. The courage to change your mind. The right to evolve without explanation.

So how do you step off the stage?

Not by deleting everything or disappearing. But by pausing long enough to ask: Who am I when no one's watching? Who am I when I stop curating?

You can start small. Post less frequently. Share something unpolished. Engage more in spaces that aren't tracked by metrics, private groups, voice messages, and in-person conversations. Let silence return between posts. Notice how it feels when you're not broadcasting.

Most of all, let yourself be inconsistent. You are not a brand. You're a person. And people are messy, contradictory, in progress. Let your online self reflect that. Not because it's a better performance, but because it's not a performance at all.

And if you ever forget, here's the simplest way to remember: log off, step outside, and do something no one will see.

Not to prove a point.

To prove that you still can.

Chapter 19: Culture in a Feedback Loop

Scroll long enough, and you begin to notice a strange sense of sameness. The language shifts, the aesthetics blur, and what once felt spontaneous begins to feel rehearsed. One day it's a meme trend, the next it's a moral stance, then a product launch, then a backlash. Ideas rise, mutate, echo, and then dissolve. All within a week. Maybe less.

Culture, once shaped slowly by tradition, dialogue, and lived experience, is now accelerated by the machinery of digital repetition. And we rarely see it happening, because we're inside it.

Every like, share, and comment is a tiny vote. A signal. Not just to the algorithm, but to the culture itself. These signals accumulate, forming patterns. The more something is engaged with, the more it's surfaced. The more it's surfaced, the more it appears to be "true," or "popular," or "relevant." And so it grows, not necessarily because it's right or wise, but because it fits the rhythm of the system.

This is the feedback loop: an idea appears, gains attention, is validated by metrics, is copied, and then amplified until it seems self-evident. But it didn't become culture because it earned it through reflection or debate. It became a culture because it resonated well with the audience.

Even memory is subject to this loop. The events that stay in public consciousness are not always the ones with the most consequence; they are the ones that generate engagement. A news story may break, circulate, fracture across opinions, become a meme, then fade. What we remember is not what happened, but what was reacted to.

This dynamic rewards intensity over nuance. Rage gets more reach than reason. Certainty gets more attention than curiosity. Irony outpaces sincerity. Complexity is flattened to a carousel post or a TikTok. And because these formats are rewarded, they begin to shape how we think.

The medium, as McLuhan said, becomes the message.

This doesn't mean people are incapable of depth; it means the system is biased against it. Slow ideas struggle in fast environments. And culture, increasingly, is built for speed.

Even personal beliefs are shaped in this loop. You may start following a creator for their humor or insight. Over time, their tone becomes familiar. You begin to adopt their framing. Not consciously, not dogmatically, just gradually. Their voice becomes part of your inner commentary. Their reaction becomes your instinct. And because the feed is tailored to reflect what you already like, you see more of the same. Your worldview is affirmed, repeated, magnified.

This is the loop reinforcing itself.

And it happens on every side of every issue. Not because people are unthinking, but because attention is finite and the system knows what keeps it longest.

The danger isn't just polarization, it's conformity. Not the forced kind, but the subtle kind. The kind that happens when we internalize the metrics of relevance and stop asking more profound questions. When we repeat things not because they are true, but because they are familiar, when we share what sounds right, we can then know if it is.

Culture, in a feedback loop, begins to cannibalize itself. Innovation becomes iteration. Dissent becomes algorithmic noise. Even rebellion gets aestheticized into a trend.

So where do we go from here?

We don't exit the loop by abandoning culture. We exit it by reclaiming our role in shaping it. That begins with attention, not just where we give it, but how we respond once we do. You can pause before you react. You can read more than the headline. You can question why something is viral, and who benefits from its virality. You can resist the pressure to comment when you haven't thought it through.

And you can choose, sometimes, to engage less.

Not because the world doesn't matter, but because you want to matter to it differently.

When you slow down, you begin to see what's real beyond the reaction. You start listening again, not just scrolling. You hear the spaces between the loud voices. You remember that not everything necessarily comes with metrics. And that silence, too, can be a kind of culture.

Because culture is not just what we consume.

It's what we contribute. And what we choose to withhold.

Chapter 20: You Were Never Meant to Be This Reachable

There was a time, not so long ago, when being unreachable was normal. You left the house, and the world didn't expect a reply. A missed call was missed. A letter arrived days or weeks after it was written. A knock at the door was a surprise. You moved through your day with a kind of privacy that wasn't considered rare. It was just life.

Now, we carry the expectation of constant availability in our pockets.

There is no such thing as a missed call anymore. There are only calls that haven't been returned yet. Messages stack up like obligations. The red dots multiply. The unread count grows. Everyone can reach you all the time, and that includes people you care about, people you work with, people who follow you, and people you've never met.

You live with a constant buzz in the background, literal and metaphorical. It's not just the device; it's the mental pressure of knowing that someone, somewhere, is probably waiting for something from you. A reply. A comment. An update. A presence.

And so you check. Again. Then again. You get back to people, not because it's a good moment, but because the space in your head is too crowded otherwise. You're managing an invisible web of invisible expectations. And slowly, your presence, the one that exists in a moment, in a room, in your body, shrinks.

Because every time you answer the ping, you step away from where you are.

This isn't a rejection of connection—quite the opposite. The impulse to be available comes from care. You don't want to leave people hanging. You don't want to be the one who disappears. You don't want to seem selfish or unkind. And so you stay reachable. Endlessly.

But the human brain wasn't built to handle this many conversations simultaneously. It wasn't built to switch between tasks, apps, voices, and time zones in rapid succession. It wasn't built to process the needs of dozens or hundreds of relationships every single day. And it certainly wasn't built to feel guilty for not being available at all times.

What gets lost in this state of constant reachability is any clear boundary between time that belongs to you and time that belongs to others.

When do you get to be truly offline, not just technically, but emotionally? When does your mind get to rest, knowing that it doesn't have to anticipate the next ping?

For many people, the answer is: rarely.

You go to bed and check one more time. You wake up and check again before your feet touch the floor. The first thing that enters your awareness is often other people's needs. And the last thing you see at night is a screen that's still updating.

This is not sustainable. Not because technology is evil, but because human beings are finite.

You are not meant to be constantly available. Not to your coworkers. Not to your social circle. Not to the entire internet. There is nothing noble about being always on. There is only depletion.

And yet, it's hard to opt out. Not just because the tools are addictive, but because they are embedded in the culture of responsiveness. We measure how much people care by how quickly they reply. We treat silence as a statement. We treat unavailability as a flaw. And so, even when you want to disconnect, it feels like you're letting someone down.

The irony is that this availability often leads to a shallower kind of connection. You're replying to everyone, but rarely connecting deeply with anyone. You're multitasking relationships. You're present everywhere and nowhere at once.

But what if being truly connected required being sometimes unavailable?

What if friendship, presence, creativity, rest, and even love depend on there being a boundary between you and the crowd?

You can start redrawing that boundary, not by vanishing, but by being honest. Tell people when you're offline. Let your autoresponder be a line in the sand. Put your phone on airplane mode for an afternoon, and let the world wait.

You're not selfish for doing this. You're reclaiming a rhythm that your nervous system needs.

Because rest is not retreat, silence is not abandonment. Unavailability is not failure.

It's the space in which you return to yourself.

And from that place, you can re-enter the world, not because you were expected to, but because you chose to.

Part III: The Human Operating System

Chapter 21: Digital Boundaries Are Emotional Boundaries

Most conversations about screen time focus on time itself, how many hours you spend, how often you check, and how long you scroll before sleep. But the deeper issue isn't just time. It's needed. Specifically, the emotional needs we are unconsciously trying to meet through devices that were never built to hold them.

If you examine your digital patterns honestly, you'll often find a kind of emotional geometry beneath them. You reach for your phone in moments of discomfort: a pause in conversation, a flare of boredom, an anxious wait, a late-night sense of loneliness. The behaviour is habitual, but it isn't random. It's often a form of self-soothing, quiet, culturally accepted, and increasingly automated.

When people say they struggle with setting boundaries around technology, they usually think they mean time limits or app restrictions. But those are surface-level tools. What they're describing is a struggle with emotional regulation. The inability to say no to a screen often stems from an inability to sit with an emotion long enough to let it pass. This is why most digital detoxes fail: they remove the outlet without addressing what was being expressed through it.

Consider the moment you compulsively check your messages, not because you're expecting anything urgent, but because a wave of unease has crept in, an argument earlier in the day, a vague fear of missing out, or simply the discomfort of not being occupied. You tap through apps looking for something that will change the state you're in. When the feed refreshes, there's relief, not because the content is nourishing, but because the discomfort was briefly covered.

This is the pattern: emotion, behaviour, distraction, relief.

It mirrors addiction psychology not in severity, but in structure. What you reach for in the digital world is often less about desire and more about avoidance. The screen becomes a shield from emotional friction. And without naming that pattern, you'll keep misidentifying the solution.

This is why digital boundaries aren't primarily technical. They are emotional disciplines. And the real work of reclaiming them often has nothing to do with the device at all.

It begins with noticing.

What emotion is present right before you open your phone? What discomfort are you avoiding when you binge on short videos at midnight? What part of your day feels so unmanageable that escape becomes the first option?

This isn't an intellectual exercise; it's a practice of honesty. Of asking what the behaviour is protecting you from, not just what it's producing.

Some digital habits are rooted in fatigue. You scroll because you're too tired to do anything else. Others are tied to self-worth. You check social media compulsively because your sense of being seen, liked, or affirmed has become tangled with it. Some habits are about grief. You seek noise to avoid sitting in silence. Some are simply about habit, but even habit has roots.

The act of setting a boundary, then, becomes less about limiting and more about listening. You're not just muting notifications; you're asking what you're trying to feel when you pick up the phone. You're not just unplugging for an hour; you're sitting with the restlessness that arises in its place and learning to understand it.

This is slow work. But it's the only kind that lasts.

Because when digital boundaries are imposed externally, through willpower, apps, and screen locks, they rarely hold. Eventually, the emotion resurfaces. The discomfort returns. And without another way to meet it, the pattern resumes. But when boundaries are rooted in clarity, when you understand what needs you've been outsourcing and begin to meet them elsewhere, then you can start to build something stable.

You might realize, for example, that you use your inbox to feel in control. Every message responded to is a small victory against chaos. But control isn't what you're truly lacking; it's rest. And if you don't learn how to rest without performance, the inbox will always pull you back.

Or you might see that your social media use isn't about distraction, but about connection. You scroll not to avoid life, but to feel less alone in it. The problem isn't the desire for connection; it's the medium you're asking to deliver it.

When you see these patterns clearly, boundaries begin to emerge not as restrictions, but as freedoms. You can choose to be unreachable for an hour, not because you're withdrawing from life, but because you're learning how to be present within it. You can close a tab without guilt because you're no longer outsourcing your worth to what might be waiting there.

This isn't about moralizing technology. It's about humanizing your response to it.

You don't need more shame around your digital life. You need a better understanding of what it represents. And once you understand, you can begin to rewire not just the behaviour, but the nervous system that drives it.

Boundaries that hold are boundaries that heal.

And healing begins with this simple truth: the phone is not the problem. It's the place you go when you don't know where else to put the feeling.

Start with the feeling.

Chapter 22: Rebuilding the Default Settings

Every device comes with default settings. Ringtones preselected, notifications enabled, location sharing quietly toggled on. Most people never change them. Not because they agree with them, but because defaults are invisible. They feel natural, even when they're not neutral. Unless you pause to examine them, you live inside them without realizing they were choices at all.

The same is true for your relationship with technology. You inherit digital norms, such as how quickly to respond to messages, when to check email, and how many times a day to scroll, without consciously deciding them. These defaults are handed to you by culture, by company design teams, by the pace of your peers. What's normal becomes what's expected, and what's expected becomes what you do. Until one day you look up and realize you're living a rhythm you never chose.

There's a moment when that realization hits, a kind of quiet unease. You notice that your phone buzzes more often than you'd like. That your calendar fills before you've even decided what matters most. Those algorithms claim your attention before you've offered it intentionally. In that moment, the myth of neutrality dissolves. You begin to understand that no part of your digital life is value-free. Everything you accept passively is shaping something actively: your focus, your mood, your day.

Rebuilding your default settings is the work of reclaiming authorship.

It starts with asking a different set of questions. Not "How do I keep up?" but "What do I want my technology to serve?" Not "What's the best app?" but "What would it mean to define enough?" Not "How do I limit distractions?" but "What deserves my attention in the first place?"

This shift is subtle but profound. It moves you from a reactive stance, one of management and control, to a proactive one of design and alignment. You're no longer tweaking the noise. You're changing the rules of engagement.

Consider how most people begin their day. The default setting is to reach for the phone: emails, news, messages, alerts.

Before you've even located your thoughts, you've absorbed the urgency of others. But that's not inevitable. That's a habit formed by design and culture. You can change it.

You can begin the day with an hour of quiet, a notebook, a walk, or a stretch. Not as a performance of virtue, but as an experiment in sovereignty. To see what it feels like to meet the day as a person, not a profile.

This principle applies everywhere. Your inbox doesn't have to be your homepage. Your social apps don't need to live on the first screen of your phone. Notifications can be silenced, badges hidden, and auto-refresh disabled. You can decide when your phone updates, not the other way around. You can stop the endless syncing, the permission loops, the nudges that disguise themselves as helpful tips.

More importantly, you can stop assuming that technology knows what's best for you.

Because most of what's called personalization is just behavioural prediction, it's not adapting to who you are, it's steering you toward what you've done before. The moment you stop and ask, "Is this still aligned with what I want?" is the moment you start reclaiming the driver's seat.

But defaults don't change all at once. They shift slowly, through small, consistent decisions.

You may choose to check your email at three set times each day. That's a new default.

You may decide that weekends are screen-free after 6 p.m. That's a new rhythm.

You may keep a paper calendar for the things that matter most, not because it's nostalgic, but because it requires more thought to commit something to ink.

Each of these actions seems simple. But they carry power because they resist the unconscious pull of the system. They say, "I will not live entirely on your schedule."

And it's not about rejecting technology. It's about re-centring the human being behind the screen.

When you rebuild your defaults, you're not becoming extreme. You're becoming deliberate. You're refusing to let the frictionless path dictate your day. And in doing so, you begin to notice how much space opens up when you stop letting tools behave like masters.

This is not a one-time reset. It's a way of living.

Every few months, reexamine the defaults. What notifications have crept back in? What apps have found their way onto your home screen again? Which rhythms are serving you, and which ones have started serving themselves?

The point isn't perfection. It's awareness. To live digitally without being governed unconsciously.

When you choose your settings, you're not just changing your phone.

You change your experience of time. You change your access to calm. You change the texture of your days, and, over time, the shape of your mind.

That's the promise of this work: not fewer distractions, but deeper alignment.

And it begins when you stop accepting the default as destiny.

Chapter 23: The One-Screen Rule

Somewhere along the way, it became normal to live across multiple screens at once. You open your laptop to answer emails, and before long, your phone is in your hand, checking a text, responding to a ping, browsing a feed while a video plays in the background. This split attention has become the invisible posture of modern life. It feels efficient. It feels productive. But what it is, what it always has been, is fragmented.

The One-Screen Rule is not a productivity hack. It's a boundary for your nervous system.

The rule is simple: at any given moment, use only one screen, and do one thing with it. Not one task across five windows. Not one device is playing audio while another runs video. Just one screen, one use, at a time.

On the surface, this may sound obvious, or maybe even unnecessary. But if you try to apply it, you'll quickly notice how rare it is to be doing just one thing with one device. Multi-screening has become the norm: laptop open, phone beside it, tablet chiming, notifications bleeding across platforms. This configuration isn't just a matter of convenience. It shapes your cognitive experience. Each added screen increases the number of attention switches, which decreases the depth of your engagement. It's not that you can't handle it; it's that you aren't meant to live inside it constantly.

Attention doesn't divide; it fractures. And with every fracture comes a cost.

What makes multi-screening seductive is its illusion of momentum. You feel busy, stimulated, in motion. You're toggling, swiping, replying. But underneath the surface is cognitive drag, mental energy lost in transitions, decision fatigue mounting silently, and memory encoding degraded. You finish the day mentally drained but unsure why, because you "didn't even do that much." This is the paradox of scattered focus: you feel overworked and under fulfilled at the same time.

The One-Screen Rule counters this not through restriction, but through clarity. It invites you to return to single-tasking, not because it's virtuous, but because it's human.

There's a neurological basis for this. The brain does not truly multitask. What we call multitasking is better described as task-switching, and each switch comes with a cost: a few tenths of a second, maybe more, during which your brain disengages from one context and reloads another. These delays are subtle, but they add up. More importantly, they compound fatigue. The more frequently you switch, the harder it is to sustain attention at all. Over time, the brain learns to expect distraction. And once distraction becomes the expectation, stillness begins to feel like absence.

The One-Screen Rule is not just about efficiency. It's about preserving the quality of your internal experience.

When you read an article with no background music, no open tabs, and no phone in view, something different happens. You begin to notice the tone of the sentences. You form mental pictures. You feel ideas unfold rather than skim across them. You're no longer scanning for highlights; you're inhabiting the thought.

Likewise, when you hold a video call without simultaneously scrolling through something else, your presence changes. You listen differently. You make room for pauses. You remember what was said. The screen doesn't need to be the enemy. It just needs to have your full attention, or none at all.

This principle can extend to daily rituals. Eat with one screen or no screen. Work on one task per device. Keep your phone in another room while writing or reading. If you're watching a film, let it be the only glowing rectangle in view. These adjustments aren't about deprivation. They are about recalibrating the pace at which your mind lives.

You may find that the One-Screen Rule feels awkward at first. Silence may feel loud. Simplicity may feel like insufficiency. But this is a temporary discomfort, a withdrawal not from screens, but from overstimulation. Once the mind readjusts, something remarkable returns: absorption. The state of being so fully engaged in what you're doing that time bends, and you forget to check anything else. This is flow, and it cannot exist in fragments.

Culturally, we've confused stimulation with satisfaction. The One-Screen Rule exposes that mistake. When you give your full attention to one thing, you experience it more deeply, and often enjoy it more. A song, when not reduced to background noise. A conversation, when not divided by scrolling. A moment, when not constantly edited by devices asking for more of you.

It's tempting to make exceptions, especially for work. But most of the time, toggling between screens in the name of productivity results in shallower work, not more meaningful output. Even in creative settings, switching between research, writing, and messaging may feel necessary, but batching those tasks rather than overlapping them often yields better thinking. Depth is not born from simultaneous inputs. It's born from sustained immersion.

The One-Screen Rule won't solve every problem. But it offers one concrete way to practice presence in a world of noise. And presence, over time, becomes the soil for focus, creativity, and rest.

There is a particular kind of peace that comes from knowing where your attention is. And there is a specific kind of power in choosing what will and will not divide it.

Start with one screen. One task. And notice what returns when the rest falls silent.

Chapter 24: Decoupling Identity From Devices

Somewhere in the last decade, a subtle but profound shift occurred. What began as tools to assist your life —phones, apps, and platforms —started to shape not just how you operate, but who you believe you are. Slowly, quietly, your sense of self became entangled with the devices in your pocket and the metrics they produced.

It didn't happen all at once. At first, the phone was just a utility. A means to stay in touch, to navigate, to remember your calendar. But then it became a mirror, a place where your preferences, opinions, photos, status updates, and playlists lived. The mirror learned to speak back. It remembered what you liked, repeated it, and suggested more. You became visible to others through it. And perhaps more dangerously, you began to see yourself through it, too.

Now, when someone asks who you are, your instinct might be to look at your screen, at the messages you've sent, the pictures you've posted, the number of unread notifications you carry like a badge. Your calendar tells you how important you are. Your social feed tells you how much you're liked. Your inbox tells you how much you're needed. The device stopped being a tool and became a proxy for your worth.

This isn't a question of vanity. It's structural.

When your digital life is the most consistent reflection of your public identity, it's easy to begin measuring your inner life against it. You might find yourself thinking in updates, crafting a tweet in your head before the moment is even over. You document not just to remember, but to prove. You keep refreshing, not because you're bored, but because each ping says, "You exist."

But who are you without it?

That's the question many people quietly avoid, because the answer can feel unsettling. Without metrics, visibility, and digital proof of presence, do you still matter? It's not a rational fear. It's emotional. It's the fear of invisibility in a world that rewards constant performance. And yet that fear reveals something crucial: you've mistaken the record of your activity for the reality of your identity.

There is no shame in having fallen into that trap. The system is built to lead you there. Everything about the modern attention economy nudges you toward visibility. You're more valuable to platforms when you're active. You're more likely to be noticed when you're consistent. You're more likely to be affirmed when you follow the expected forms. And so you keep showing up, but you also keep feeling a quiet, gnawing exhaustion that comes from maintaining an identity instead of living one.

Decoupling your identity from your devices doesn't mean abandoning the digital world. It means remembering that you are more than the sum of your notifications, more than the profile you've shaped, and certainly more than your screen time report.

You are a person who forgets, who doubts, who changes, who grows. And most of that evolution happens offline, without documentation.

There are parts of you no one will ever see, not because you're hiding, but because they don't belong on display. Your attention to a friend's grief. Your unspoken anxieties. Your early morning ideas that never leave the notebook. These are no less real because they're not public. They are, in fact, the most real. And they exist regardless of whether your phone is turned on.

Reclaiming that understanding requires a kind of digital untangling.

You can begin by noticing how often your identity is reflected to you through a metric. Do you feel differently about a post depending on how many people responded to it? Do you reframe your experiences, so they'll be more shareable? Do you check analytics, not because it changes what you'll do, but because it feels like validation?

Then ask: what part of me is looking for approval here? What need is being outsourced to a machine?

Once you see it, you can begin to shift. Not by deleting everything, but by practicing selfhood in spaces that aren't constantly observed.

You can go for a walk without sharing it. Write something without posting it. Celebrate a moment without recording it.

These aren't acts of disconnection. They are acts of remembrance, a way to remember that your life has value even when no one is watching.

You can also resist the urge to measure every effort. Just because a message gets fewer likes doesn't make it less accurate. Just because fewer people see your work doesn't mean it lacks impact. Reach is not a synonym for worth. It's simply one measure, among many, and often the least meaningful.

The truth is that your deepest values, the things that shape your character, don't translate easily into content. And they shouldn't have to. You are allowed to be multi-dimensional, inconsistent, and evolving. You're allowed to contradict your last post. You're allowed to change your mind.

Because you are not a brand. You are not your feed. You are not your inbox. You are not your phone. You are someone living a life that can't be fully captured in pixels. And when you reclaim that truth, the digital tools stop defining you and start serving you again.

Chapter 25: Your Nervous System Is the Filter

Before any notification reaches your mind, it touches your body. Long before you form thoughts about your screen time, before you open your email, before you even register that a buzz has occurred, your nervous system has already begun to respond. The digital world doesn't just shape how you think; it shapes how you feel at a physiological level. And most of that influence happens below the threshold of awareness.

We tend to treat technology use as a cognitive issue. We talk about productivity, distraction, and attention spans. But your relationship with devices is first and foremost a relationship with your body's state. If your heart races every time your phone lights up, if your stomach tightens when your calendar loads, if your breathing shifts subtly when you open a social app, that is your body speaking before your brain has a chance to interpret.

This matters. Because no matter how sophisticated your boundaries or intentions are, you cannot think your way out of a dysregulated nervous system.

At its core, your nervous system is designed to scan for safety. Constantly and unconsciously, it asks: Am I okay right now? That question is answered not with logic, but with sensation. If you're calm, your system opens to the world. You breathe more fully. You listen. You stay grounded. But if your body senses overwhelm, even if the stimulus is something as small as an unanswered text or an overflowing inbox, it begins to contract. You don't always feel panic, but the system tightens. You become more reactive, less reflective. You start to respond to inputs, not from clarity, but from a desire to resolve the tension as quickly as possible.

And this is precisely the state most digital environments cultivate.

Because they are built on urgency. Red badges. Pings. Numbers are climbing or stalling—visual cues designed to keep you scanning. Even in moments of apparent stillness, the underlying cues stimulate the nervous system. There is always something you might be missing. Something you might need to fix. Some status that needs attention. Your body absorbs this long before your mind catches up.

This is why screen fatigue isn't just about blue light. It's about vigilance. Your body is held in a low-grade state of alert throughout the day, reacting to stimuli that never fully resolve. That reaction has a cost on your energy, your ability to focus, your quality of sleep, and even your mood.

You might find yourself exhausted at the end of a day where you sat in place, barely moved, and never encountered a significant crisis. That exhaustion isn't imagined. It's the consequence of hours spent in a subtly activated state, navigating dozens of digital interactions that never allowed your system to settle fully.

Reclaiming a healthy digital rhythm, then, requires learning to filter your screen use through the nervous system, not just the calendar or the to-do list.

This means asking a different kind of question: not "How much time did I spend online today?" but "What state was my body in while I did?"

Was I calm when I opened that email, or bracing? Did I pick up my phone out of boredom, or because I felt unsafe in silence? Was I using this screen to connect, or to escape something uncomfortable in my body?

These questions aren't moral. They're diagnostic. They reveal not what's wrong with you, but what needs support.

Once you begin listening to your body in this way, specific patterns become impossible to ignore.

You notice, for example, that certain apps leave you feeling jittery, while others don't. Checking the news in bed can subtly but consistently disrupt your sleep. The fact that Zoom meetings are stacked too tightly together compresses your breathing. That switching tabs constantly makes it harder to finish anything at all, not because you lack discipline, but because your body never fully returns to baseline between tasks.

This awareness creates choice, not in the sense of strict limits or cold abstinence, but in the sense of alignment.

You can begin to space your tasks with recovery in mind, not just productivity. You can turn off notifications not because they're annoying, but because your body isn't meant to be startled twenty times an hour. You can decide not to check your messages during meals, not out of rule-following, but because your digestion and your presence improve when your system isn't anticipating interruption.

These aren't lifestyle hacks. They're acts of restoration. Ways of signalling to your nervous system: you are allowed to be here. You are not being hunted. You don't have to solve everything right now.

The more you live this way, the more you'll notice that your digital habits aren't just behaviours. They are feedback loops between the environment and your biology. When those loops run unchecked, they lead to burnout. But when those loops are grounded in awareness, they can become stable again.

Technology can support your nervous system if you're the one setting the pace. A guided meditation app can lower your heart rate. A voice message from someone who knows how to listen can settle your nerves more than any feed ever could. A podcast played during a walk, not while juggling tabs, can bring rhythm instead of overstimulation.

But the technology won't decide that for you. Only you can.

And the best guide you have is already built in. Not in your settings. Not in your notifications. But in the part of you that knows how to breathe deeply. The part of you that loosens when the screen dims. The part of you that says, clearly and without urgency: this is enough.

Chapter 26: Tech Isn't the Enemy, Overuse Is

If you've ever felt the impulse to toss your phone across the room or fantasized about moving off-grid, you're not alone. At some point, nearly everyone has reached a moment of digital exhaustion so intense it feels like the only solution is complete escape. And yet, after a few days offline, sometimes even a few hours, you reach for the very tool you swore off. Not out of failure, but out of recognition: you still need it.

Technology is not the villain in this story. It never was.

The phone, the apps, the platforms, and the interfaces are inventions. They are tools. And tools, by definition, are neutral until given a purpose. A hammer can build a house or break a window. A camera can preserve memory or distort it. A calendar can help you live with intention or fill your days with pressure. The morality of a tool depends on its use, not its existence.

What makes technology feel oppressive isn't the fact that it exists. It's the degree to which it invades spaces it was never meant to control. The problem is not your calendar app; it's that your calendar runs without pause, seven days a week. The problem is not your email; it's that you feel compelled to check it when you should be asleep. The problem is not your screen; it's that it's become your default escape, your entertainment, your anchor, and your mirror, all at once.

Overuse, not existence, is the issue.

This distinction matters because it changes the shape of the solution. If tech were the enemy, the answer would be elimination. But if overuse is the problem, then the answer is containment. Not rejection, but boundaries. Not abstinence, but intention.

Consider how you relate to something like food. You don't demonize it when you overeat. You recognize that the body needs nourishment, but also that it can be overloaded. You learn, ideally, to eat what energizes you, not just what distracts or numbs. The same principle applies to technology. It is something to be used consciously, with attention to rhythm and portion, not something to be eradicated.

And like food, the experience of using tech should leave you with a clue. Do you feel drained or restored afterward? Has it expanded your perspective or narrowed it? Has it left you more connected to yourself and others, or just more stimulated?

The reason this kind of discernment is difficult is that the line between useful and overused is constantly moving. What was once a tool for writing becomes, with just one click, a rabbit hole of distraction. What began as a platform for expression morphs into a scoreboard for your identity. You open your phone to do one thing and surface thirty minutes later, disoriented and slightly ashamed, without having done the thing at all.

But this doesn't mean the tool is to blame. It means design features hijacked your attention, you didn't choose, and rhythms you didn't author. And that's where the work begins, not in shame, but in redesign.

The question becomes: what do you want this device to help you do? If it's to stay connected, then which connections matter most? If it's to stay informed, then how much information is enough? If it's to support your creativity, then are you spending more time consuming or creating?

Once you name the purpose, you can build the boundary. You can keep your tools close, but your purpose closer.

You can silence most notifications, not out of rebellion, but out of clarity. You can move social apps off your home screen, not because you hate them, but because they don't need to be within thumb's reach every moment of the day. You can replace compulsive opening with deliberate checking. You can schedule screen-free hours not because it's trendy, but because your mind needs unstructured space to function well.

These changes aren't aesthetic. They're neurological. Every time you use a digital tool in a way that aligns with your intention, you strengthen the neural pathways associated with that alignment. You reduce the likelihood of unconscious drift. You preserve energy that would otherwise be lost in transitions. Over time, you experience your tools not as extensions of pressure, but as extensions of choice.

This is the fundamental shift: moving from unconscious use to conscious command.

Because no platform, no matter how addictive its design, is stronger than your attention once you learn to own it. And no algorithm, no matter how aggressive, is more powerful than a human being who knows what they want and why they're here.

That's the truth buried under all the noise: technology doesn't have to be escaped. It has to be reclaimed.

Reclamation doesn't require massive life changes. It requires small, repeated acts of sovereignty.

Deciding not to open your email before breakfast. Leaving your phone in another room while you write. Choosing not to respond instantly when something can wait.

These are not moral statements. They are spatial ones. They give your inner world room to exist before the outer world floods in.

And when you make enough of those choices, your nervous system starts to trust you again. It stops bracing. It stops waiting for the next ping. It stops treating the screen like a threat disguised as necessity.

It remembers what your mind forgot: that technology is yours to use. It was never meant to use you.

Chapter 27: Digital Minimalism, Reimagined

The phrase "digital minimalism" has come to evoke a particular kind of aesthetic: grayscale home screens, deleted apps, abandoned platforms, and extended personal essays about breaking up with the internet. To some, it sounds clean and admirable. To others, it is severe and unrealistic. But whatever image it conjures, it often carries an unspoken premise: less is better. Always.

This binary is both limiting and misleading.

Digital minimalism, if it is to be sustainable, cannot be defined solely by what you remove. It must be determined by what you return to. Subtraction may begin the process, but it cannot carry it out. The long-term success of a minimalist approach doesn't depend on how little you use, but on how you've chosen what remains.

This is the difference between austerity and alignment.

Austerity often emerges from burnout. You hit a point of exhaustion or disgust and respond by clearing the deck entirely. You delete the apps, mute everything, and cancel the subscriptions. For a few days or weeks, this feels liberating. But soon the needs that prompted the tech use resurface. The desire to connect, to learn, to share, to organize your life. And if those needs don't have new outlets, the old ones return. Maybe slower, maybe disguised, but they creep back in.

This is not failure. It's physiology. The brain doesn't simply let go of habits because you tell it to. It requires replacement, not just removal. The same is true for attention. It needs direction, not just silence.

That's where a reimagined minimalism begins, not with rejection, but with rebuilding.

At its core, digital minimalism is not about being less digital. It's about being less passive. It's about replacing compulsive use with conscious structure. It's not about deleting the internet. It's about choosing how and when you allow it into your life, and being honest about what it costs.

For example, if you spend two hours a day on social media, the question isn't whether that's "too much." The question is:

what are you getting for those hours? Are they enhancing your life, or simply filling it? Are they lifting your thoughts, or looping them? Are they offering the connection, or the performance of it?

Minimalism that works doesn't declare war on technology. It reasserts your agency inside it.

This might look like turning your phone from an open field into a curated room. You don't remove every tool; you remove the ones that clutter the space. You don't mute everyone; you prioritize who deserves front-row access to your attention. You don't try to do everything through one device; you specialize your tools to their best use.

You might decide, for example, that your phone is for communication and music, but not for browsing news or social media. Your laptop is for creative work, not personal admin. That your tablet is for reading, not for watching. These decisions aren't arbitrary. They create functional clarity. They help your brain associate each tool with a specific kind of energy.

The goal here isn't asceticism. It's clarity of use.

When everything does everything, you end up living in a state of ambient distraction. But when things have their place, physically and functionally, you reduce the cognitive load of decision-making. You don't have to wonder whether to scroll, reply, check, or post. You know what this tool is for, and what it's not.

This is the principle behind reimagined digital minimalism: intentional architecture.

Architecture that supports rhythm, not rigidity. That allows you to engage without being engulfed. That's flexible enough to adapt, but structured enough to hold.

This isn't about going offline. It's about going online with a purpose, and leaving when that purpose is met.

It means you can use social media without becoming a version of yourself tailored for it. You can use email without living in it. You can watch videos without being pulled into a feed that decides what you should want next.

It means asking yourself, not once but regularly: What is the role of technology in the life I want to live? Not the life I'm tolerating. Not the life others expect. But the life I want. The one where presence is possible. Where focus feels natural. Where time stretches again.

When you ask this honestly, minimalism stops being a project and starts becoming a posture. A way of moving through the digital world with eyes open and pace restored. A refusal to let design defaults dictate the quality of your inner life.

You don't have to throw away your phone. You don't have to disappear. But you do have to choose. And then choose again tomorrow. Because clarity, like attention, is a daily act.

Chapter 28: Rethinking Convenience

Convenience has become a modern god, worshipped not with temples or rituals, but with every tap, swipe, and click that makes something a little faster, a little easier, a little more seamless. It's hard to argue against it. After all, who would choose difficulty over ease? Why wait when you can have it now?

But convenience has a hidden cost. And it rarely sends a receipt.

The promise of technology has long been framed in terms of efficiency: fewer steps, less friction, more output. And on the surface, this promise has been delivered. You can order food without speaking. You can move money with a fingerprint. You can summon a car to your exact location, get weather for your precise street, and receive news tailored to your exact worldview. All of it instantly, without interruption, without effort.

But ease is not the same as depth. And frictionless is not the same as fulfilling.

Over time, when you outsource every inconvenience to a screen or a system, something unexpected happens. You stop engaging fully with the world that gave rise to those inconveniences in the first place. You lose a kind of sensory contact with life. The inconvenience, it turns out, was not always a flaw. Sometimes, it was the doorway to meaning.

Please think of the conversations we've edited out in the name of speed, those small exchanges with baristas, clerks, strangers in waiting rooms. Think of the meandering walks that became rideshares. Meal kits have replaced the cooking experiments. The mental math exchanged for calculators, the memory replaced by search, the journey replaced by GPS. None of these things is evil. They save time. But what happens to a person, or a culture, when the accumulated result is that no action demands your full participation?

Convenience begins as a gift. It becomes a habit. Eventually, it shapes your expectations of reality.

You grow impatient with anything that doesn't respond instantly. You become allergic to effort that isn't immediately rewarded. You resent silence because it offers no feedback. You treat your time as too valuable to spend, but somehow still feel like you're losing it. And the more you design life for ease, the harder it becomes to tolerate anything else.

This is the paradox of convenience: it expands your capacity while shrinking your tolerance.

Technology isn't to blame for this. It's simply delivering what it was asked to provide. But the ask itself has gone largely unexamined. Somewhere along the way, we began treating convenience as synonymous with progress. We assumed that faster meant better. That simpler meant smarter. That effortlessness was always an upgrade.

But not all difficulties are wasteful. And not all ease is good.

Cooking a meal from scratch is more complicated than ordering it, but it can also bring you into your senses, your hunger, and your home. Writing by hand is slower than typing, but it forces your mind to engage differently with language and thought. Navigating without a map app can be frustrating, but it anchors you in place, in time, in memory. The effort is not a flaw. Sometimes, it's the very thing that makes the moment feel alive.

When convenience replaces these efforts wholesale, you may not notice what's gone missing until you try to engage deeply again and find yourself restless, distracted, and oddly detached. Not because you're broken, but because you've been conditioned to expect reality to arrive at the pace of a screen.

Reclaiming your relationship with effort doesn't mean rejecting all convenience. It means discerning where it serves you and where it steals from you.

It begins with the simplest of questions: What am I gaining, and what am I losing?

When you save ten minutes with an app, what do you spend that time on instead? If that time is spent on rest, reflection, and connection, then the convenience may be serving its purpose. But if that time is filled with more scrolling, more noise, more passive consumption, then the trade might not be worth it.

Not every moment needs to be efficient. Some moments need to be inefficient on purpose.

You can choose, for example, to walk when you could ride, not out of moral superiority, but because walking gives your brain space to think. You can cook when you could microwave, not to prove anything, but because the process slows your mind and settles your nervous system. You can memorize a friend's number, not because you need to, but because it reminds you that memory has value, even now.

This isn't nostalgia. It's resistance to the idea that everything worth doing must be made frictionless.

Because convenience, left unchecked, does something subtle to your sense of agency. It makes the world seem like something you consume, rather than something you participate in. It turns experience into a transaction. And it flattens the parts of life that were never meant to be optimized.

Grief, for instance, is inconvenient. So is love. So is learning, and parenting, and healing, and creativity. None of these things moves quickly. None of them offer shortcuts. But they are the substance of life. If you can't tolerate inconvenience, you'll struggle to live in any of them for long.

So the invitation is not to make life harder for its own sake. It's worth noticing where effort invites you back into presence. It's to reintroduce slowness not as punishment, but as a portal. It's to see that what you call inconvenience might be intimacy in disguise.

Because sometimes, the thing that takes longer is the thing that leaves you feeling more human when it's done.

Chapter 29: The Right to Disconnect

For most of human history, absence was ordinary. You left work, and work stayed behind. You left town, and no one expected to reach you. You entered a conversation, and nothing else interrupted. You were either with someone, or you weren't. You were either reachable, or you weren't. The boundary between presence and absence was clear, not always honoured, but at least visible.

Now, the line is gone. And with it, a vital human right has begun to erode: the right to be unreachable without explanation.

We are, in a technical sense, always available. The phone is with you. The inbox is synced. The messages accumulate while you sleep. And so absence now requires justification. People say "sorry for the delay" after just a few hours. They apologize for not responding instantly, for missing a ping, for not noticing a comment. The baseline expectation has shifted. Being online isn't just a possibility; it's a presumed posture.

But what's often called connection is, in practice, just persistent availability. And the more consistently you are expected to show up digitally, the more your right to proper rest begins to disappear. You become a node in a network that never powers down. You carry the weight of constant partial attention, always somewhere else in your mind, even when your body is trying to relax.

This is not sustainable. And more importantly, it's not neutral.

Constant availability isn't just inconvenient; it's an extraction of mental labour. Your cognitive presence is now something that can be mined at any hour, by anyone with your number, your handle, or your email. Your thoughts, your replies, your attention, these are resources. And when the expectation is that you're always "on," those resources become fair game.

But here's the deeper cost: when you always have to be reachable, you stop knowing what it means to be fully with yourself.

The right to disconnect is not a luxury. It's a boundary that makes clarity possible.

Without it, you may still be productive. You may still function. But you will rarely drop into deep presence. And over time, that shallowness becomes self-reinforcing. You check your phone because you feel slightly off, and you feel slightly off because your mind has no refuge. You become reactive, irritable, and tired, but you don't connect it to the constant reactivity, because it's just "normal life."

To reclaim your right to disconnect is to say: I do not exist only in response to others. I am allowed to have time that belongs to no one else. Not my employer. Not my audience. Not even my friends and family. Just me.

This is not selfish. It is a necessary condition for renewal.

And it's not about ignoring people. It's about re-establishing a rhythm that includes space for recovery, not just for output. A rhythm that respects your nervous system's need to idle. A rhythm that sees stillness as part of the work, not a break from it.

Disconnection does not mean disappearance. It means sovereignty.

You get to choose when to step back, and how.

That choice might look like not checking email after 6 p.m., not replying to texts during dinner, and not feeling obligated to explain why you didn't answer right away. It might look like building regular time offline into your schedule, not just on weekends or vacations, but woven into the architecture of your ordinary life.

It might mean creating digital exit rituals, such as turning off notifications when your workday ends, putting your phone in a drawer for a stretch of unstructured time, walking without headphones, or letting your mind wander without input.

The mechanics are simple. The challenge is cultural.

Because we don't just fear missing out, we fear being seen as missing. We're afraid of falling behind. Of seeming inconsiderate. Not responding quickly enough in a world that moves at the speed of light. And that fear keeps us tied to our devices not just by habit, but by identity. We believe that being responsive is a form of responsibility. To be reachable is to be relevant.

But your worth is not measured by your speed. And your presence is not validated by your availability.

To disconnect is to remember this. It is to return, not to less, but to enough.

In some countries, the right to disconnect has begun to enter legal conversation, with workers protected from after-hours messages and expectations curtailed by statute. But legislation alone cannot restore what was taken by culture. This right must also be reclaimed at the personal level, not in isolation, but as part of a broader rethinking of what it means to be well in a digital age.

You do not owe the world constant access to your time, your thoughts, or your attention. You are allowed to shut the door, not only physically, but digitally. You are allowed to pause before responding. You are allowed to take your time.

And perhaps most importantly, you are allowed to be missed. Because only when it's possible to be absent can your presence regain its weight.

Chapter 30: Redesigning Your Digital Home

Every device you use has a home screen. But few people ever stop to ask a simple question: Is this a home I want to live in?

The answer is often no, not because the technology itself is broken, but because the environment it creates has been passively inherited. You download an app, and it lands wherever the operating system decides. You accept default notifications, default folders, and default layouts. You start your day inside a digital space that was never really yours. It's organized for access, not intention. For convenience, not clarity.

Over time, this environment begins to shape your behaviour. What's easy to reach becomes what you check first. What's visible becomes what you value. What's noisy becomes what you respond to. The structure of your digital home starts determining the rhythm of your real one.

You wouldn't tolerate this kind of design in your physical life. You wouldn't place a blaring television in the center of every room, or scatter piles of unopened mail on the floor. But this is precisely what most people live with on their devices. And because it's virtual, we underestimate how much stress it creates. We assume it's just "part of modern life."

But like any space, your digital environment reflects your priorities, or distorts them.

Redesigning your digital home isn't about making it minimalist. It's about making it intentional. It's about crafting a space that serves your mind rather than hijacks it. A space that reflects who you are, not just what the market wants you to want.

You begin by noticing what takes up space, visually, cognitively, and emotionally.

The first thing many people see when unlocking their phone is a grid of apps they didn't choose with care. Social media front and center. Messaging next to email. A dozen icons, all competing for attention. Some have unread badges. Some are blinking. Some are open by muscle memory. And before you've made a single conscious choice, you're already reacting.

That first glance sets the tone for the entire interaction.

But what if your home screen were quieter? What if it held only the essentials, tools you use deliberately, not compulsively? What if opening your phone didn't drop you into a marketplace, but into something that supports your focus, or even stillness?

You don't need a complicated system. You need space.

Space between stimuli. Space between functions. Space that gives your mind a moment to arrive before being pulled in.

This means removing apps that serve no purpose other than filling time. Not because they're evil, but because you don't want your free moments always defaulting to scrolling. It means silencing badges and hiding notification previews, because every number you see pulls your attention forward, before you've even decided where it belongs.

Your digital home should not be a hallway filled with ringing phones.

It should be a front porch, a space that invites clarity, not confusion.

Email, for example, doesn't need to be your first screen. If it's not where you want to live your day, don't put it on your doorstep. Group similar apps together and move them to the second page, or into folders with intentional names: "Intentional Use," "Mindless Use," "Work Only." Not as rules, but as reminders.

Redesign is not about discipline. It's about architecture.

You are much more likely to use your tools well when the environment encourages the behaviours you want. And the inverse is just as true: when the environment is chaotic, your attention will be, too.

This principle applies beyond layout. Your digital home includes your inboxes, your feeds, your cloud storage, and your calendar. All of these spaces need maintenance, not to look neat, but to function without friction.

Decluttering is not just about deleting. It's about asking, again and again: Is this still serving me?

That newsletter you never read. That app you haven't opened in months. The digital workspace is cluttered with tasks from projects that are no longer relevant. None of these things is wrong in isolation. But collectively, they act like ambient noise. They fill the edges of your vision and erode your cognitive energy.

We underestimate how much clutter taxes us, because we never deal with it all at once. But it accumulates. And each time you see it, your mind has to make a decision: engage, ignore, or return later. Each micro-decision adds weight to the day.

You can remove that weight.

Not in one sweeping overhaul, but through consistent, quiet pruning.

Five minutes a day to delete what doesn't matter. Ten minutes a week to reorganize what does. One hour a month to reflect on what needs to change. Not as a project, but as a rhythm. Because a digital home, like any home, stays livable only if it's maintained.

And when it is, something shifts. Your device stops feeling like a portal to chaos. It becomes an extension of your clarity. You open it without bracing. You close it without guilt. You begin to trust that the space you've built will not pull you away from your values the moment you enter.

This is what redesign offers. Not a cleaner screen, but a clearer life.

Because when the space around you is shaped with care, the mind inside it can breathe again.

Part IV: The 30-Day Mind Reset

Chapter 31: Week 1 – Awareness and Audit

Before you can change your relationship with technology, you need to know what that relationship is.

Not what you think it is. Not what you wish it were. Not what others tell you it should be.

Just what it is, honestly, right now.

That is the work of Week One, not deletion, not detox, not restriction, but observation. You aren't here to shame yourself. You're here to witness how you live when no one's watching. And what you discover may not match what you imagined. Most people are surprised when they finally look.

Because the story we tell ourselves about our tech use is almost always neater than the reality. We claim to "just check Instagram a couple of times a day," yet our usage log reveals 47 pickups, each lasting a minute or two, which is enough to reset our attention but not satisfy our desire. We say we only check email "in the morning and afternoon," but it turns out we glance at it seven times between 10 a.m. and noon. We claim to be great at focusing, but we can't recall the last time we worked for an hour straight without reaching for our phone.

The modern digital experience is full of these gaps between perception and practice. And bridging that gap begins not with guilt, but with clarity.

For the next seven days, your only goal is to become a calm observer of your digital life. Not a judge. Not a reformer. Just someone willing to look at what is, without rushing to fix it. That pause is powerful. It interrupts the shame cycle. It allows something deeper to surface: curiosity.

Start with your attention. When do you first reach for a screen each day? Not when you intend to, but when you do. Is it before you've spoken to anyone? Before you've gotten out of bed? Before you've taken a breath not mediated by input?

Then look at your rhythms. When does your usage spike? What time of day do you feel most pulled toward checking?

When does your focus break? When do you scroll out of habit, not hunger?

Next, observe your mood. How do you feel after fifteen minutes on your favourite app? After ten minutes in your inbox? After skimming headlines for a while? Not what you think you're supposed to feel, but what your body registers. Tense jaw? Shallow breath? A vague sense of rush or restlessness? This is your nervous system's report card.

The point isn't to change anything yet. The fact is to see.

And not just the visible behaviours, but also the hidden drivers.

For many people, screen time isn't about the content. It's about regulation. You reach for your phone when you're bored, lonely, uncomfortable, or anxious. It offers immediate distraction and, with it, temporary relief. But that relief comes at a price: it interrupts a conversation you didn't let finish.

This week is about listening to that unfinished conversation.

When you notice yourself picking up your phone, pause for a breath. Ask, not with critique, but with gentleness, what emotion was present just before you reached? What were you avoiding? What were you trying to soothe?

You don't need to answer these questions perfectly. You need to let them open the door.

The more often you do this, the more you'll begin to notice something astonishing: your digital behaviours are not random. They are patterned. They are shaped by emotion, context, time of day, energy levels, and cues in your environment. They follow rhythms, loops, triggers. And once you see the loop, you are no longer inside it without choice.

That's what an audit is, not a spreadsheet of guilt, but a map of your current operating system. You are gathering data, not for punishment, but for design. You can't rebuild your relationship with technology if you don't understand the blueprint you're starting from.

Some people like to write down their findings. Others pay closer attention throughout the day. There's no one right way. What matters is that you're looking. And that, even in looking, you're doing something most people never do: stepping outside the automatic.

There is an enormous difference between reacting and choosing. But the difference can only be felt if you slow down enough to witness your behaviour as it happens.

This week, that's the only task. Watch your habits. Notice your defaults. Name your patterns. Don't edit. Don't hide—just notice.

No version of this audit makes you a "better person." The audit is not for others. It's not even for your future self. It's for the part of you that's ready to live more consciously now. The part that's tired of being led by loops it didn't create. The part that knows attention is a finite resource and wants to use it well.

When you start from awareness, you begin not from resistance, but from self-trust. And that trust is the foundation of sustainable change.

So for this week, forget willpower. Forget fixing. Forget cutting anything out.

Just watch. Let yourself see, with gentleness and honesty, how you live in this digital life of yours. Not because you've failed. But because you're finally ready to see the whole picture before you decide what to change.

Chapter 32: Day 3 – Emotional Triggers

Not every screen habit is logical. Most aren't.

You don't open an app because it was the best thing to do at that moment. You open it because something inside you needed a change in feeling. A tension to ease. A sensation to fade. A certain silence to end.

That's the truth most digital behaviour conceals: it's not about the content; it's about the emotion underneath.

You may scroll when you feel uncertain. You may refresh your inbox after receiving criticism, hoping the following email will dilute the discomfort. You may reach for your phone in a waiting room because stillness makes you anxious. You may check the news compulsively when you're overwhelmed, mistaking information for control.

These are not character flaws. They're coping patterns. And once you start seeing them, you can begin to understand what you're asking your phone to do.

Today is about noticing those emotional triggers. Not in general. In real time.

When your hand reaches for your phone, pause for just one breath. Interrupt the motion. Let your hand hover. Ask: What was I feeling just before this?

Maybe it was boredom, the low-grade restlessness that comes with gaps in stimulation. Maybe it was loneliness, that sudden pang of being with yourself and not knowing what to do with your own company. Perhaps it was anxiety, a vague worry you didn't want to name. Or stress, disguised as "just needing to check something quickly."

It might even be something more challenging to admit: envy, resentment, sadness, shame. Feelings that are difficult to hold, especially without distraction. Feelings that make your body want to escape, and your phone offers the quickest way out.

You don't need to fix the feeling. You don't need to change it. You need to name it.

Because once it's named, it can't run the show from behind the curtain.

For most people, this practice alone, just noticing the emotional cue, creates a tiny wedge of choice where none existed before. The pause becomes a portal. You realize: I don't have to open the app. I don't have to soothe this right now. I can feel it. I can let the wave crest. I can stay by myself.

This is not about avoidance. It's about capacity. The more you build the capacity to stay with discomfort, the less power those unconscious loops will have over your behaviour. Your nervous system learns: we can be here. Even with this. Even now.

This doesn't mean you never reach for your phone again. It just means that when you do, you know why.

Because behind every compulsive digital habit is a need that hasn't been met in a better way.

Sometimes that need is for comfort. Sometimes for reassurance. Sometimes just for rhythm, to break up the shapelessness of an hour that feels empty.

And none of those needs are wrong. But they will not be fully met by devices designed for stimulation, not nourishment.

So, when you feel the trigger, when you sense yourself reaching not out of purpose but out of emotion, try waiting ten seconds before acting. Not to test yourself. Not to prove anything. To see what happens when you stay present.

Ten seconds is enough time to notice if the urge was about the app or the feeling.

Sometimes, the feeling will dissipate on its own. Sometimes, you'll realize you were looking for connection and might benefit more from a walk, a call, or a few quiet breaths. Other times, you'll go ahead and check your phone, but you'll do it with awareness, not compulsion. That's the shift.

You're not becoming a different person. You're becoming more fluent in your internal cues.

And in that fluency, you begin to regain authorship.

What was once automatic, becomes intentional. What was once numbing becomes visible. What was once noise becomes a signal.

None of this happens overnight. But Day 3 is where it begins in earnest, when you stop measuring digital habits purely by time and start exploring their emotional architecture.

Because the goal here isn't just fewer hours on your phone, it's a life where your feelings don't need to hide behind pixels.

It's a life where you can sit with what's real, and let your technology follow your needs, not dictate them.

Chapter 33: Day 5 – The Phantom Vibration Test

There's a moment many people experience that sounds almost fictional, until you realize how common it has become. You're sitting quietly, perhaps in a meeting or reading or driving, when you feel it: a buzz. You check your phone. Nothing. You check again—still nothing. You begin to question whether it even happened at all.

This is the phantom vibration.

A hallucinated sensation, usually on the leg or near the hip, that mimics the vibration of an incoming message. And it's not just an odd quirk. It's a physiological clue. It reveals something more profound: your body has begun to anticipate digital input even when it isn't there.

On Day 5 of the reset, you're invited to pay attention to these moments. Not just the false alarms, but the real ones too, the way your body responds when your phone lights up, even before you know what it says. Your shoulders rise. Your stomach tenses. Your breath shallows. A message is not just a message. It's an event.

Why?

Because most of us, consciously or not, have trained our nervous systems to interpret the phone as a source of urgency. We don't wait to find out if it's essential. We react as if it were always that way. And over time, that edge, of readiness, of response, gets built into our bodies, until even silence starts to feel like suspense.

The phantom vibration is not a failure of imagination. It's the result of a loop that's run too many times.

You hear the ping. You get the hit. You react. Repeat. Eventually, your brain doesn't need the ping to trigger the anticipation. It does it on its own. The association is strong enough that even the *possibility* of a message is enough to spark physical alertness.

This has nothing to do with addiction in the moral sense. It's about conditioning. Just as a dog salivates at the sound of a bell in Pavlov's experiment, your body begins to prepare itself at the mere idea of incoming data. You're not addicted to your phone. You're trained to expect it.

Day 5 is about reversing that training.

Not with force, not with judgment, but with curiosity. The test isn't about getting a phantom buzz. It's whether you can notice it, pause, and gently ask: What part of me is bracing right now?

That question matters because most of us don't realize how much of our daily tension is tied to this invisible anticipation. We walk around not just reacting to what's on our screens, but pre-reacting to what *might* be. The brain doesn't always distinguish between a real stimulus and an expected stimulus. If your body is prepared for interruption, you're already halfway distracted, even if the message never comes.

This state of ambient tension costs you more than you realize. It erodes your baseline calm. It fragments your presence. It makes it harder to enter and sustain deep focus. It turns every quiet moment into something haunted by the next vibration.

And worst of all, it feels normal.

That's the power of the test. It brings the unconscious to the surface. It helps you name what your body has adapted to without your consent.

When you feel a phantom vibration, or even a real one, see if you can take a single breath before responding. One inhale. One exhale. Just long enough to create a sliver of space between the stimulus and the response. Just enough room to remember that not everything demands your attention. That not every sensation is a summons.

Then, if you do reach for your phone, do it with intention. Ask: What am I hoping this will say? What feeling am I looking to resolve? What outcome am I preloading into this check?

You won't always know. But asking makes you more conscious. And that consciousness, over time, begins to break the loop.

You may even experiment, for part of today, with silencing your device entirely. Not forever. Not even all day. Just long enough to observe your body's reaction to the absence of signals.

Do you feel relief? Or anxiety? Do you forget about it altogether? Or check compulsively?

There's no correct answer. The point isn't perfection. It's an observation.

Because what you're doing here is learning the shape of your alertness.

You're discovering how tightly your sense of safety or control is tied to digital responsiveness. You're learning whether your attention is something you give, or something that gets taken the moment your phone moves.

You might find that phantom vibrations decrease with silence. Or that they spike when you first turn off alerts. You might find they vanish when you're immersed in real connection or deep focus. You might be surprised by how much space opens up when the body is no longer bracing for input every few minutes.

Whatever your discovery, let it be enough.

This is not a problem to solve. It's a pattern to become intimate with.

Because once you can feel the way your attention has been conditioned, once you can witness the residue of all those pings, you begin to see your phone for what it is again: a tool, not a tether.

And maybe, just maybe, you start to believe something else too.

That not every buzz is your business. That not every vibration is a verdict. That silence, too, is a kind of power.

Chapter 34: Week 2 – Clear the Clutter

If the first week of this reset was about seeing clearly, the second is about making space.

The audit has done its job: it's pulled your unconscious habits into the light. You've seen the emotional triggers, the autopilot loops, the pull of the phantom vibration. Now, you're ready to begin a different kind of work, not intellectual, but architectural.

You're going to begin clearing the clutter.

This isn't about deleting every app or stepping off every platform. It's not about turning your life into a clean white slate. It's about removing the digital noise that clouds your thinking and fragments your attention. It's about subtracting the pieces that no longer serve your values so that the ones that do can stand in clearer relief.

And most importantly, it's about doing that slowly, deliberately, not out of frustration, but with a kind of quiet respect for what you're reclaiming.

Start not with your phone, but with a question: What kind of mind do I want to live inside?

Is it spacious? Or crammed? Does it feel like it has oxygen? Or does it feel like it's always catching up?

Your digital life has a direct bearing on that answer. Because clutter isn't just about things, it's about friction. And the more friction there is between your attention and your intention, the more fatigued you become.

Every unnecessary app, unread notification, redundant inbox, or broken workflow is a tiny source of friction. A point of confusion. A decision waiting to be made. And while none of them may seem urgent, they add up. Every single one is a tap on the shoulder of your brain, asking for just a little bit more bandwidth than it deserves.

So, this week, you begin letting those taps fall silent.

You begin by simplifying.

Start with the most immediate digital environment: your phone.

Look at your home screen. Is it calm? Or crowded? Are the things you value most, creativity, reflection, and connection, visible and supported? Or are they buried beneath noise?

Now is the time to move things. Not because they're evil, but because you want to choose your defaults instead of inheriting them. Move low-value apps to the second screen, or to a folder you title honestly, like "Time Fillers" or "Things I Check Without Meaning To." Name them not to judge, but to disarm. Truth is a form of resistance.

Then turn to notifications. This is one of the single most impactful changes you can make, not dramatic, but profound.

Ask yourself: which notifications truly deserve to interrupt you?

You may find that the list is shockingly short. Messages from a loved one. A calendar alert for a critical meeting. Maybe an app that supports your well-being. Beyond that, the rest are often echoes of someone else's priorities.

You are not required to leave every channel open. You are allowed to take yourself off call.

As you go, pay attention to how your body responds, not just your mind. When the screen becomes calmer, does your breath deepen? When the buzzes disappear, do you feel an exhale you didn't realize you'd been holding? These physical cues matter. They're the signals that your system is beginning to trust you again.

From here, extend the clearing into your digital workspaces.

Your inbox: is it a tool, or a trap? Do you open it with clarity, or with dread?

Try unsubscribing from five things you don't read. Archive what you know you'll never revisit. Create a folder titled "Not Now," and sweep the digital debris into it. Not to hide it forever, but to relieve your brain of the burden of triaging the same messages day after day.

Next, look at your files, your desktop, and your bookmarks. Are they organized to reflect how you think now, or how you thought five years ago?

Don't aim for perfection. Just aim for lightness. The fewer decisions you have to make to find what matters, the more energy you have for real thinking.

Finally, examine the flow of input into your mind.

This is the invisible layer of digital clutter, the media, headlines, memes, videos, messages, and alerts that pass through your consciousness without your explicit consent.

Ask: What do I let in every day? And what do I get back for that attention?

If the answer is a little more than stimulation, then you are feeding your brain calories without nourishment. You're full, but not sustained.

You don't have to disappear from the internet. But you do need to prune.

Unfollow sources that leave you feeling anxious or envious. Mute feeds that distort your attention. Create new rhythms for checking the news, rather than grazing all day. Let your curiosity be deliberate, not reactive.

As you do this, you may feel some discomfort. There's often a strange guilt that comes with creating space, as if silence needs defending.

But this discomfort isn't a sign that something's wrong. It's a sign that you've been living under a spell: the idea that to be engaged means to be constantly stimulated. Every open tab is a form of presence; clicks measure that productivity.

Clearing the clutter shows you another way. A slower, steadier rhythm. A home for your attention, not a hallway for everyone else's demands.

And once the clutter recedes, even a little, you start to feel what was there all along: the presence beneath the noise. The focus that didn't need to be built, only uncovered.

That's what this week is about. Not discipline. Not aesthetic. But the quiet courage to live in a mind that has room to think again.

Chapter 35: Day 10 – Notification Blackout

There are few modern sounds as intimate as the one your phone makes when it needs your attention. A buzz, a chime, a ping. It doesn't matter the tone; it cuts through whatever moment you're in and carries a quiet urgency: "Something is happening. Come look."

And so you look.

You always look. Because even when you try not to, the anticipation lingers. A slight shift in posture, a glance toward the device. It's not just that your phone called for you, it's that you've been trained to believe something important might be on the other side.

The notification has become one of the most underestimated forces in modern life. It looks like a feature. It functions like a behavioural script. With each tap, your brain receives a reward, or at least a resolution. Curiosity is scratched, uncertainty is ended, and your attention resets.

Today, we test what life feels like without any of that.

For just one day, you are going to turn off all non-essential notifications. No red badges. No preview popups. No banners dropping from the top of your screen while you're doing something else. Not even vibrations.

Just silence.

This is the notification blackout.

At first, it may feel disorienting. You'll unlock your phone and find nothing waiting for you. No signal of what to check. No suggestion of what to feel. The familiar drip-feed of information will stop. And in its place, something even more unfamiliar will appear: space.

That space is not empty. It is filled with potential.

Potential to follow your thought to the end of a sentence. To finish a task without breaking eye contact with your attention. To be present in a conversation without wondering if you're missing something. To walk, or sit, or read, or think, with no one else's urgency whispering in your pocket.

This is not about asceticism. It's about recalibration.

Because when every app has permission to notify you, your day is no longer yours. It belongs to the loudest bidder. You can no longer trust that your attention is responding to your actual priorities. You're being prompted into action by software designers who have no idea what matters most to you today.

You don't need to demonize the technology to acknowledge this truth. Notifications are not malicious. They're just indifferent. They are designed to capture, not to care. That's your job.

Which is why this blackout matters. Because it reveals just how much of your mental rhythm is being shaped by forces you didn't consciously invite.

Maybe you open your phone to check the time and end up on Instagram. Or you see a badge on your calendar, and suddenly you're inside your email app. Or you feel a buzz and reach for your device without even realizing it was your smartwatch, not your phone, that triggered the sensation.

These aren't flaws in your character. They're predictable outcomes of a system that feeds on interruption.

And they can be changed.

But not by willing yourself into better habits. Habits are downstream from the environment. First, you change the conditions, then you observe the behaviour that follows.

So today, change the conditions.

Turn off the alerts—everyone who isn't tied to actual urgency. Ask yourself: what must interrupt me today? What can wait until I'm ready?

You'll find the list is shorter than you thought.

The rest, the notifications about comments, likes, promotions, updates, newsletters, flash sales, "someone just went live", can wait. They were always going to stay. You didn't know you had permission to let them.

Now you do.

As the day goes on, pay attention not just to your behaviour, but to your body. Does your jaw unclench? Does your breath deepen? Does your thinking stretch a little farther before it's interrupted?

You may notice something else too: phantom tension. The feeling that you *should* be checking something. The subtle anxiety that comes not from missing out, but from missing the chance to respond. This, too, is part of the pattern being broken. The impulse to stay updated at all times is not a desire for connection; it's a strategy for managing discomfort.

The discomfort of not knowing. Of being left out. Of being behind. Of being seen as unavailable.

But you are not a server. You are a person. And people need recovery.

Recovery from the cognitive strain of context switching. Recovery from the emotional drain of being perpetually "on." Recovery from the compulsive pacing of attention shaped by pings instead of presence.

A single day without those pings reminds you: the world still turns. You didn't miss anything that you couldn't wait for. Most of what wants your attention is not urgent. It's just loud.

The silence of this blackout is not a punishment. It's a return. A return to the possibility that you might decide how you spend a moment, rather than being drafted into it.

You are not unreachable. You are simply self-directed.

And tomorrow, when you decide what notifications to re-enable, you'll do so from a place of clarity, not habit. You'll choose the ones that capture your attention, not steal it.

Because the point of this reset was never disconnection for its own sake, it was to make space for the parts of you that still know how to live without being prompted.

Chapter 36: Day 12 – Slow Feeds and Real Reads

There's a strange kind of hunger that builds over time when your mind lives on a fast feed. You scroll, you swipe, you sample. Each post, each headline, each notification arrives like a bite, momentarily satisfying, then instantly replaced. The meal never comes. The hunger never leaves.

What's being starved isn't just your intellect. It's your depth.

Today is about feeding it differently.

You've already begun to clear space, notifications are reduced, and inputs are quieted. Now you get to decide what re-enters that space. And not all content is created equal. Some of it rushes through you like sugar, and some of it invites you to sit down and think. Some of it jolts—some of its roots.

This chapter isn't about turning you into someone who reads the great books or deletes every social feed. It's about reawakening a different rhythm of attention, one that can stretch, reflect, and absorb. One that gives your nervous system a break from twitchy, bite-sized content and instead introduces you to ideas that take time.

We could call it slow media. Or longform. Or deliberate reading. The label doesn't matter. What matters is the shift in how you take in information.

Most people today consume content the same way they consume chips, unthinkingly, reflexively, with no end until the bag is empty or something more interesting comes along. The feed is designed this way. It's endless on purpose. Its goal isn't for you to feel informed; it's for you to stay. And to stay, you must be perpetually unsatisfied.

But slow content asks something else of you. It asks for your presence. It doesn't rush to reveal its meaning. It doesn't promise stimulation every six seconds. It builds. And in building, it reminds you what your brain is capable of when it's not being split in thirty directions.

Today, you're going to reintroduce this experience, even briefly.

Pick something, an essay, an article, a book chapter, that stretches beyond 500 words. That unfolds, rather than explodes.

That offers one idea instead of twenty. Something that doesn't blink or animate or demand interaction, but waits to be read.

Set aside 30 minutes—no background noise. No alerts. Let the text be the only thing you're doing. If that feels uncomfortable, notice that discomfort. Stay with it. That discomfort is the residue of a mind learning to come home to itself.

This will not be easy at first. Your attention may resist. It has grown used to leaping, not landing. The part of your mind trained by scrolling will itch for movement, for novelty. That's okay. Let it pass. Keep reading.

You may not even remember what this kind of attention feels like. The ability to read four or five pages without interruption. To enter the logic of someone else's thinking. To let your mind echo back with thoughts, questions, surprises. This isn't nostalgia. Its capacity. And it's still yours.

The reward doesn't come in the first paragraph. It comes after. In the shift from surface-level stimulation to cognitive immersion. In the experience of reading not as consumption, but as dialogue.

The best slow content doesn't merely inform. It alters your interior. It reshapes how you see, not just the topic, but yourself about it. That's not something a reel or a tweet can do. Not because those formats are inherently shallow, but because they are built for speed, not depth.

This isn't an argument against digital media. It's an argument for digital nourishment.

You can still have your feeds. But what if you thought of them the way you think of snacks, not bad, but not the foundation of a healthy mind?

The real question becomes: What would it mean to make slow thinking a regular part of your life again?

To read something in full, rather than skim. To revisit an argument instead of replacing it with a new one. To underline. To pause. To finish.

This is what most of us long for without realizing it. A way of engaging that isn't just about staying updated, but about being moved.

You don't need to do this every day. But once a week. Once a weekend. A single hour set aside for a longer read, or a longer listen, or a longer watch, something that doesn't compress itself to fit the feed.

And once you've had that experience, you begin to see everything else differently. The urgency fades. The scroll feels shallower. The input feels louder. Not because the world changed, but because your capacity just reawakened.

This is how we reclaim attention, not through restrictions, but through remembrance.

You don't need to escape technology to think deeply. You need to change the pace.

And sometimes, all it takes is one long read to remind you: your mind was built for more than skimming.

Chapter 37: Week 3 – Rewire the Loop

By now, something subtle has started to shift.

The silence of notifications has made more space in your day. You've seen the triggers behind your most reflexive screen use. You've cleared out digital clutter, and your attention has felt, at moments, lighter. Not always. But enough to notice the difference between reacting and choosing.

Now comes the more challenging, quieter part: replacing the old loop with a new one.

If you stop at subtraction, removing distractions without reimagining what belongs in their place, the old habits will return. Maybe not tomorrow, perhaps not next week, but soon. Nature, and your brain, both abhor a vacuum.

That's why Week 3 isn't about cutting anything else. It's about constructing something in its place.

Every screen habit is a loop, trigger, behaviour, and reward. It's a cycle you've followed hundreds, maybe thousands of times. You feel bored. You open a feed. You get a flicker of stimulation. You think briefly better. Your brain logs the sequence. Repeat.

These loops aren't personal failures. They're efficient systems. Your brain is trying to help. It sees your discomfort and offers a reliable escape. And because that escape "works" in the short term, the loop becomes automatic.

What we rarely ask is whether the reward is real or just familiar.

This week is your chance to build new loops. Not by force. Not by guilt. But by using the very same mechanism: create a trigger, choose a new behaviour, and experience a reward that nourishes rather than numbs.

Start with your attention peaks, those times of day when you most often reach for distraction. Maybe it's late morning, when motivation dips. Or mid-afternoon, when fatigue creeps in. Or late at night, when your mind wants stimulation without effort.

Instead of trying to will yourself away from your phone, prepare something to move toward. A new loop. Something simple, repeatable, satisfying, not because it overstimulates, but because it anchors.

This might involve stepping outside for three minutes of sunlight, journaling a few lines, or putting on music and resetting your space. Or doing nothing for five minutes, literally nothing.

At first, your brain won't believe it's a better deal. It's used to the sugar rush of screen time. But if you stick with it, the reward changes. You begin to feel the difference between being soothed and being sedated. And something inside starts to prefer the former.

One of the most overlooked truths about digital habits is that we rarely replace them with things we truly enjoy. We try to stop cold. We remove the dopamine but don't replace the ritual—no wonder the old patterns return.

Rewiring the loop doesn't mean becoming a monk. It means offering your brain something better than scrolling, something that leaves you more whole, not less.

Even your physical environment matters. If your phone is always in arm's reach, it becomes the default response to any unfilled moment. So, part of this week's work is environmental. Keep your phone in a drawer while working. Leave it behind when you go to lunch. Charge it in another room overnight. These are not acts of restriction. They're acts of rebalancing. You're making your intentional behaviours easier to reach than your reactive ones.

You'll also find power in pairing new habits with old cues. For example, if you always open social media after checking email, insert a pause there. Place a sticky note with a single question: "What do I need right now?" It sounds small. It is small. But so is the habit it's interrupting, and so it fits.

Eventually, your new loops will begin to feel natural. Not because they've overwritten the old ones entirely, but because they've grown strong enough to compete.

And the rewards, while subtler, run deeper.

After finishing a walk, you feel clear instead of scattered. You journal for five minutes and leave with insight instead of inertia. You sit in stillness and discover that not every discomfort needs solving.

Your brain learns. It adapts. It begins to prefer the rituals that don't leave you drained.

This is what makes change sustainable, not discipline, but design.

You are not at war with your screen. You are building a new alliance with your attention. One that respects your need for ease but doesn't sacrifice depth to get there. Because the goal isn't just to use your phone less.

The goal is to eliminate the need to manage every moment. The goal is to remember you have other ways to reset, to cope, to center. The goal is to make room for a different kind of life.

One loop at a time.

Chapter 38: Day 17 – Your Focus Block

Focus isn't a mood. It's a practice.

We tend to think of it as something that either shows up or doesn't, something we catch in a good moment, or chase when we've fallen behind. But in truth, focus is rarely spontaneous. It requires space. And not just mental space, but temporal, physical, and emotional space too.

Today, you'll begin giving it that space on purpose.

It's time to build your Focus Block.

Not a productivity hack. Not a race to output. A block of time carved out and protected for doing something with depth, something that matters, something that requires your full attention, even if it's just for 90 minutes.

The exact number doesn't matter. The structure does.

This block exists for one reason: to give your brain a chance to stretch. Not sprint, not flinch, not scroll, but stretch, into sustained engagement with a single thread of thought, effort, or creativity. Whether it's writing, problem-solving, coding, planning, studying, or designing, the outcome is the same. What matters is that you choose one thing and let it have the room to unfold.

In a typical digital day, this rarely happens. Even your best intentions are interrupted by the buzz of incoming messages, calendar alerts, browser tabs, and internal pings of "just for a second" distractions. Each one is small. But the damage is cumulative. Not because the interruptions take so much time, but because they break the mental momentum needed to delve deeper.

Your brain operates in rhythms, not rigid units. One of the most powerful of those rhythms is called the ultradian cycle, a natural 90- to 120-minute window in which cognitive performance peaks, followed by a necessary period of rest or reset. We're not meant to stay focused indefinitely. But we *are* built for sustained bursts of undistracted effort, when we honour that window with the right conditions.

That's what the Focus Block gives you. A dedicated period that aligns with this rhythm and allows your mind to settle into flow. Not the buzzy, romanticized version of flow. But the actual, grounded process of going from fragmented to fully engaged.

To do this well, you'll need more than just time on a calendar. You'll need a signal. A ritual. A way of crossing the threshold from reactive mode into presence.

It might be a physical cue, closing your door, lighting a candle, putting on a specific playlist, silencing all notifications, or placing your phone out of sight. It might be something internal, such as three deep breaths, a phrase you repeat, or an intention you write down. These aren't superstitions. They're environmental anchors. They tell your brain: now we go in.

And once you begin, the rule is simple: one task only. Not five tabs. Not switching between projects. One focus.

In the beginning, this will be harder than it sounds. Your brain, accustomed to novelty, will look for exits. You'll feel the phantom urges, check this, open that, respond to something. Let them pass. They are echoes of a previous rhythm, not commands.

And if you break the block, because something truly urgent arises or your focus falters, don't treat it as failure. Treat it as data. What interrupted you? What pulled you out? What can you adjust next time to reduce friction?

That's the point: not perfection, but pattern.

Most people go months, sometimes years, without ever experiencing 90 uninterrupted minutes of thinking. Their days are ruled by reaction. But this block is different. It's not about efficiency. It's about reclaiming what scattered input has taken from you: the ability to follow a thread to its end. To finish a thought. To complete something that matters before your mind gets co-opted.

And when you do?

There's a satisfaction no feed can match.

It's not loud. It's not addictive. It doesn't demand applause. But it's real. You feel it when you close your laptop, not depleted, but clear. You feel it when you finish a page or solve a problem and realize: you were *here* for it.

That feeling is what makes the practice sustainable. Not the outcome, but the state.

And over time, as you repeat this rhythm, maybe not every day, but regularly enough, it becomes something more than just a block. It becomes a sanctuary.

A space in your week where the rest of the world doesn't dictate the pace. Where urgency waits at the door. Where your mind is not something you manage, but something you inhabit fully.

If that sounds rare, it is. But it doesn't have to be.

You don't need to wait for permission. You need to protect the conditions. Because focus isn't a luxury, it's a basic human rhythm.

And in a digital world that feeds on distraction, carving out this rhythm, on your terms, is nothing short of an act of creative resistance.

Chapter 39: Day 20 – The Phone Fast

You learn the most about a relationship when you step away from it.

Today is that step.

By this point in the reset, you've done more than surface-level work. You've audited your behaviours, observed your emotional patterns, cleared digital clutter, and begun to rewire your habits. You've made space for deep attention. You've turned off the noise and replaced it with new rhythms. And now, you're ready to go one layer deeper.

For the next 24 hours, you'll set your phone aside.

Do not just silence it. Not just turn off notifications. You'll put it away, out of reach, or at least out of sight, and go without it for a full day.

This is your phone fast.

And before you rush to justify why it isn't possible, pause.

It's true, there are lives, jobs, and roles that depend on reachability. Parents, caregivers, doctors, dispatchers, and other key personnel must stay available. But availability is not the same as accessibility to everything, all the time. Even if you need to be reachable for one or two specific people, the rest can wait. They probably already are.

This fast is not a moral exercise. It's not punishment. It's a diagnostic. A way to feel the shape of your attention when the default tool for distraction, stimulation, and regulation is no longer in your hand.

You may feel fine. Or you may feel disoriented. Most people feel both.

The first few hours are usually the hardest, not because anything is missing, but because the body still expects to be interrupted. You may find yourself reaching for something that isn't there, like tapping a phantom pocket. That gesture is revealing. It shows you how often you've been using your phone as a response to boredom, uncertainty, discomfort, or just habit.

And then something else happens. The world slows. Not in a way that's always pleasant. At first, the quiet may feel too quiet. You may feel itchy for input. You may find your thoughts less edited, less managed. They come and go with a kind of rawness you forgot existed. The moments between tasks stretch a little. There is more space than you're used to.

That space is not a void. It's a mirror.

Without a phone, you notice how many transitions in your day are usually filled by screens. Walking from one room to another, waiting in line, sitting at lunch, and lying in bed. Each of these tiny moments has been colonized by scrolling. And now, without that option, they come back into focus.

You begin to see your environment again. You hear more. You pause longer. You eat more slowly. You notice the people around you, not just as background figures, but as human presences with their own pace and weight. You see yourself, too, how often you want to distract, how rarely you truly rest.

Somewhere in the middle of the day, a question will arise: What exactly was I avoiding by being so constantly available?

Not just to others, but to input, in general.

You might not have an immediate answer. You don't need one. The value of this fast isn't in naming the problem, but in experiencing the reset. You're stepping out of a loop, not to escape reality, but to observe it without interruption.

And then, slowly, the anxiety starts to settle.

Your nervous system, no longer bracing for the next ping, begins to trust the rhythm of the moment. You feel less compelled to fill the gaps. You remember how long an hour can feel. You remember what it's like to follow one train of thought to its conclusion without someone else's agenda sliding across your screen.

You remember, in short, what it's like to live without being summoned.

This memory is the point. Not because digital life is inherently bad, but because most of us haven't felt the contrast in so long, we've forgotten there was ever another way to experience time.

The phone makes that contrast visible. And from it, you gain perspective not just on your habits, but on your needs. You begin to notice which parts of your screen feed you, and which fill the space where your real life was meant to unfold.

The point isn't to give up your phone forever. The fact is to return to it with intention.

When the 24 hours are over and you power the device back on, do it slowly.

Notice what rushes back in. The flood of messages. The stack of updates. The tiny pulse of urgency in your chest. Ask yourself, in that moment: how much of this is mine?

And then make a choice, not a grand gesture, but a quiet one.

Maybe you turn off one more category of notifications. Consider moving a distracting app out of reach. Perhaps you decide that you'll protect one day each week for a slower presence. Or maybe you make a habit of pausing before you open anything, asking, "Do I need this right now, or do I just want not to feel what I'm feeling?"

That question alone can change your relationship with your device.

Because you're not trying to go back in time, you're just trying to stop outsourcing every moment of discomfort to a screen. You're remembering that your mind belongs to you, even when the phone is on. And that, sometimes, the most radical reset is also the simplest:

Put it down. Walk away. Let your attention breathe.

Chapter 40: Week 4 – Integration for Life

You've cleared the clutter. You've silenced the noise. You've rewritten some of the most reflexive loops in your day. You've even gone a full 24 hours without the device that has followed you almost everywhere for the last decade.

And now, the most important part begins.

Not detox. Not retreat. Integration.

Because it was never about removing the phone, it was about recovering your mind. And that recovery only becomes durable when it's woven into your real, unfinished, sometimes chaotic life.

This final week is not the end of the reset. It's the beginning of your relationship with technology on new terms, ones you authored.

And the first thing to accept is this: you will drift.

That's not failure. That's gravity. Your work, your friends, your culture, your news, your professional identity, they all pull you back toward the surface. Toward the buzz, the scroll, the shortcut. And you will return to it, sometimes without meaning to. You'll open the feed you forgot you muted. You'll re-download an app you once deleted. You'll reach for your phone in a moment of fatigue and catch yourself mid-swipe, wondering how you got there.

Let it happen.

Then, come back.

Because the reset was never meant to turn you into someone who never slips, it was meant to give you a new center of gravity, so that when you drift, you know where home is.

Integration is the quiet art of returning and returning to your rhythm and returning to your attention and returning to your values, even in a world that's designed to scatter them.

And returning begins with recognizing the signs that you're leaving yourself again.

For some, it's cognitive: the feeling that thoughts are piling up without structure. For others, it's emotional: restlessness, irritability, the low-grade dissatisfaction that follows hours of shallow stimulation. Sometimes it's physical, tight shoulders, tired eyes, an unease you can't quite name. Whatever your signal, learn it. Let it become a prompt, not for guilt, but for grounding.

The second principle of integration is that sustainable change is built on rhythm, not rigidity.

You don't need a perfect system. You need one that can breathe.

That might mean designating one evening a week as screen-free, not because it's idealistic, but because it gives your mind one stretch of silence. It might mean keeping one app off your home screen permanently. It might mean continuing a 90-minute Focus Block every morning, and or checking email only during set hours. These are not laws. They're scaffolding, enough structure to support your intention without becoming a cage.

And you'll know the rhythm is working not because you never crave distraction, but because when you return to presence, it happens more easily. Less resistance. Less negotiation. Just a gentle shift back to where you meant to be.

That's how you know your nervous system is healing.

Third: remember what's yours to protect.

Your attention is not neutral. What you focus on becomes how you feel, how you think, and eventually, who you are. The feed you scroll, the messages you absorb, the pace you live at, these are not incidental. They become the architecture of your inner life.

And so protecting your attention is not a matter of productivity. It's a matter of self-respect.

You are allowed to choose slowness. You are allowed to say no to urgency. You are permitted to go quiet. You are allowed to make your inner state the thing you tend to first.

Because when the collective current no longer owns your mind, you start to think your thoughts again. And from there, everything changes.

That doesn't mean isolation. It means discernment.

You don't have to delete everything. You have to decide what earns your presence.

Not every message deserves an instant reply. Not every update needs a glance. Not every moment is a good one to open your inbox. Not every voice online needs to be heard in your head. You can choose. You've proven that already.

Finally, remember that integration is never an arrival.

There is no finish line.

There is only the ongoing practice of attention, messy, imperfect, and profoundly human.

You will forget. You will override your own rules. You will spend two hours online doing nothing you intended to do. And still, the next moment is yours. The next breath is an invitation.

This reset wasn't about control. It was about contact. Contact with the parts of you that still know how to be present. How to feel. How to reflect. How to create without an audience. How to listen without multitasking. How to read a page and absorb it. How to spend an afternoon without checking anything.

That version of you isn't ideal. It's already here.

You just needed to make room for it.

So as you move into the final part of this journey, into the long-term vision of a digital life that supports your actual one, take this with you:

You are not behind. You are not late. You are not broken for having been distracted. You are simply a person, remembering how to come back to yourself.

And now you have a path.

Part V: A New Kind of Digital Life

Chapter 41: Life After the Ping

There comes a moment, often quiet and unmarked, when you realize the world isn't going to tell you when to be done.

There is no final ping, no gentle fade to black. No voice will arrive to say: "You've seen enough for today." No alert will whisper: "You may return to yourself now."

Technology is a rhythm without an end. It loops, refreshes, and reloads. Its language is urgency; its grammar is repetition. And in that endlessness, it teaches you to forget your own internal pace. Your sense of when to stop, when to rest, when to look up.

But what happens when you stop listening for the ping?

What happens when you no longer need it to punctuate your time, your thoughts, your worth?

That's the question of this next chapter, not metaphorically, but literally. What does it mean to build a life where your nervous system doesn't brace for the following notification? Where silence isn't suspicious, and downtime isn't failure?

It doesn't mean you'll never be interrupted again. Of course not. The world is full of obligations and noise. But there's a difference between being interrupted and living in a state of constant readiness for interruption. That second state, the anticipatory flinch, the vigilance, the ever-scanning for something to respond to, is what this chapter invites you to release.

The shift doesn't happen instantly. You don't just uninstall a behaviour pattern that took a decade to build. But slowly, the body begins to trust again. The absence of a ping becomes less eerie. You stop compulsively checking. You start finishing your thoughts. You realize you don't feel as tired at the end of the day, not because you worked less, but because you weren't splintered into dozens of micro-reactions.

In place of that splintering, something unfamiliar arrives: continuity.

You begin to notice that a morning without alerts feels different from one spent managing fragments of other people's needs. You see the power of a single, undisturbed task. You rediscover the natural arc of focus: a beginning, a middle, a completion.

Without the ping to dictate your attention, your priorities become visible again. Not the ones in your inbox, but the ones inside your life. The unfinished project you kept postponing—the conversation you haven't had. The book you've started and restarted so many times, it now just marks your guilt. Without digital noise, you're left with the hum of your actual life, and its requests are quieter, but more lasting.

This isn't always comfortable.

There are moments when the silence is louder than you expected. When the stillness feels empty. You reach for the phone, not to learn or connect, but to avoid. To soften the sharpness of just being still with yourself. That's okay. We've all built habits around avoiding boredom, uncertainty, and loneliness. The device didn't create those feelings, but it did offer a convenient exit from them.

Life after the ping means choosing not to take the exit every time it appears.

And that changes more than just your screen time. It changes your relationship with discomfort. You start to believe you can sit with something without immediately solving it, that you can feel tired and not override it with stimulation. That you can be uncertain and not resolve it with a scroll.

This is not a withdrawal. Its growth.

Your nervous system adjusts. You stop bracing for the buzz. You no longer need the digital nudge to feel awake or entertained. Instead, you develop a different relationship with presence. A steadier one. One less contingent on the next thing.

And perhaps most surprisingly, life after the ping doesn't feel like deprivation. It feels like clarity.

There's less noise in the room. Your thinking slows, but in a good way. Conversations lengthen. Tasks complete. Time stretches again, the way it did before everything became so compressed and clickable.

You stop measuring your day by how much you managed to consume, and start measuring it by how much you managed to experience.

This is a form of liberation. Not from devices entirely, but from dependence on them to regulate your sense of worth, pace, and urgency.

When the ping no longer dictates your internal clock, you begin to reclaim the calendar of your actual body, your rhythms of energy, your intuition, your focus, your rest. You learn when to pause because *you're* tired, not because the battery is low.

Of course, the devices will still be there. The pings can always be turned back on. The world won't stop asking for your attention. But now, you have a choice.

And choice is everything.

Not just the choice of what to use, but the deeper one: when, how, and why.

When you stop living in reaction to the ping, you start living for your life.

You begin to listen for other signals. Your breath. Your fatigue. Your thoughts. Your child's voice. Your desire to step outside for no reason at all. And you respond, not instantly, but deliberately.

That's what this whole reset has been about.

Not restraint. Not restriction but reorientation. A return to a life where your attention is not simply divided among apps, tabs, alerts, and feeds, but anchored in something quieter, something more lasting.

Yourself.

Chapter 42: Joy, Not Judgment

You don't need to feel bad to make a change. And yet, so often, digital minimalism has been sold as a moral correction, as though using your phone less makes you more virtuous, and every notification you respond to is a failure of character.

But shame is a poor architect for lasting change.

This chapter is your invitation to reframe your journey, not as penance, not as retreat, but as joy. As freedom. As a movement toward something richer, not an escape from something corrupt.

Because if you carry judgment into your relationship with technology, it will only deepen the rift between what you do and what you think you *should* do. It creates a double burden: the behaviour itself and the guilt that follows. And over time, that guilt turns the whole project of digital wellbeing into yet another performance, another source of stress, another arena for failing to be "good enough."

The truth is, you don't need to feel guilty about using your phone. You don't need to perform mindfulness. You don't have to justify your tech boundaries with academic studies or inspirational language. You don't need a philosophical treatise to back up your instinct to close the laptop and go for a walk.

What you need, what most of us need, is permission to choose joyfully.

To choose a slower day because it feels better, not because hustle is evil. To mute the group chat because your brain needs quiet, not because you're superior for ignoring people. To step away from the feed because you want to, not because you've concluded it's toxic.

Joy is a more sustainable fuel than guilt.

And yet, for many people, the moment they begin creating boundaries, they also start making a narrative: that they are now somehow more intentional, more awake, more "real" than those who remain enmeshed in the system.

This, too, is a trap.

Because superiority is just another performance. One that doesn't deliver the calm or presence it promises. It only replaces the noise of distraction with the noise of ego. And that noise can be just as exhausting.

The goal here is different. It's softer. It's more human.

To find the places in your digital life where lightness lives. Where creativity returns. Where your thoughts aren't constantly curated, monetized, or measured. Where the mind slows, and the self gets quieter, not out of obligation, but relief.

And you know that feeling. You've tasted it. Maybe after a long walk without headphones. Or a meal shared with someone where no one picked up their phone. Or a weekend afternoon when you forgot to check your messages and realized nothing fell apart.

Those moments were not moral victories. They were simply beautiful.

That's the feeling worth returning to.

Because when presence becomes associated with pressure, when every act of logging off feels like a statement, you begin to resist it. You stop seeing it as refuge and start seeing it as work. But presence, at its best, is not work. It's a homecoming.

And the more you return to it, not because you "should," but because it feels *good*, the more naturally it becomes your default.

This shift also changes how you relate to others.

You stop policing how your partner uses their phone. You stop judging your friend's social media habits. You stop comparing your "digital purity" to someone else's daily scroll. Because you realize: everyone is negotiating their version of presence. Everyone is seeking relief from overwhelm in the ways they know how.

When you lead with judgment, people defend themselves. When you lead with joy, they soften.

If someone sees you step away from the noise and you're lighter, clearer, more at peace, not holier, they may start to wonder what that space feels like for themselves.

And that's the quiet power of this reset. Not that it makes you better, but that it makes you freer. And freedom is contagious.

It opens up the possibility that there's another way to be with technology. One rooted not in detachment, but discernment. One where the phone becomes just a phone, not a portal, not a tether, not a test.

That kind of relationship doesn't require you to opt out of modern life. It only asks that you stop outsourcing your self-worth to it.

So let this next phase be grounded in joy.

Let the app you delete be one you don't miss. Let the feed you unfollow make room for something more nourishing. Let the evening you spend offline be one filled with slowness and laughter, not restraint and self-righteousness.

Let the quiet be a relief, not a performance. Let the decision to log off be like opening a window, not closing a door, because the point was never to prove anything.

The point was to feel more alive.

Chapter 43: Digital Sabbaths

There is a reason almost every ancient culture developed rituals of rest. Not just sleep, but complete rest, rhythmic, collective pauses that punctuated the noise of the everyday with silence, slowness, and stillness.

They understood something we've almost forgotten: that life without interruption is not a luxury. It's a necessity for staying whole.

In a digital world, that interruption looks different. It doesn't come from work in the fields or from the demands of physical labour. It comes from constant access, perpetual reachability, relentless input, and a subtle, unending expectation always to be just one tap away from everything and everyone.

So the idea of a Sabbath returns. Not as doctrine. Not as dogma. But as a digital practice. A rhythm of refusal, not to abandon modern life, but to remember that you are allowed to step outside of it for a while.

A Digital Sabbath is not a punishment. It is not an act of moral superiority. It is not a rebellion. It is simply a choice to pause.

For one day, or part of a day, each week, you set the devices aside. You unplug not to make a statement, but to return to yourself. To the people in front of you. To the thoughts that don't need to be shared. To the moments that don't need to be captured.

This isn't about escaping the world. It's about remembering what it feels like to belong to it again.

And the first time you try it, it might feel strange. Your hand may reach for your phone more than you'd like. Your mind may twitch with curiosity: What's happening? What have I missed? The void of input may feel uncomfortable.

Let it be.

That discomfort is the very reason the practice matters. Because in that space, you reencounter yourself, not the curated, performing version of you, but the quieter one. The one who doesn't refresh anything, who doesn't wait for a reply, who doesn't perform her worth through productivity or visibility.

That version of you is always there. She's just been buried under pings and expectations.

And over time, something else begins to happen. The silence deepens—the pressure thins. The day stretches.

The hours feel wider than you remember. You look at the clock and realize it's still only noon. You feel the difference in your breath, in your focus, in your body. There's no background tab running in your mind. You are where you are.

You may even feel something like awe.

Awe, not in the spiritual sense, though it could be that too. But awe as in: "I forgot life could feel like this." That time could pass without checking anything. Those meals could end without anyone pulling out a phone. That rest could be accurate, uninterrupted, and complete.

This rhythm, the weekly return, is what transforms everything you've practiced so far into something lasting.

Because habits can slip, routines change. Work ramps up. Life throws its chaos. But when you carve a day, any day, even half a day, as untouchable by digital noise, you build an anchor.

And anchors don't need to be big to hold.

They need to be steady.

You don't have to call it a Sabbath. You can call it "a reset," "a no-screen Saturday," or simply "my off day." The name is not the point. The pause is.

The point is not to follow a rule, but to live in rhythm. To create contrast. To remember, regularly, what it feels like to be undisturbed, not once a year, but every week.

Some people set firm boundaries. Phones off at sundown. No work messages until Monday. No social media all weekend. Others keep it looser. No scrolling until noon. No TV until after dinner. No apps that pull them into loops.

What matters is the intentionality with which you approach each day. That your mind knows this day has a different texture, a different weight.

Because that difference is what your attention craves.

That difference is where recovery lives.

And over time, the Digital Sabbath stops being something you "should" do and becomes something you protect fiercely, not out of guilt, but out of love for what it gives you.

You start to look forward to it. You begin to build the rest of your week around it. You notice the way your mind prepares to settle into it. You feel the pull of it when you've gone too long without one.

It becomes not just a reset, but a ritual. A place you return to again and again, not to escape life, but to remember how to inhabit it fully.

Because the world doesn't need more perfectly optimized, digitally fluent people. It requires more present ones. People who can pause. People who can rest. People who know how to hold silence without filling it.

A Sabbath, digital or otherwise, is not an act of fragility. It is an act of strength. A declaration: My attention is mine. And one day a week, I will not trade it.

Chapter 44: Designing a Brain-Friendly Life

You can't control the internet. You can't filter out every distraction. You can't make the world stop buzzing, scrolling, updating. But you can design your environment to work with your brain instead of against it.

That's the foundation of a brain-friendly life.

Not a perfect life. Not a minimalist utopia. Just one that reduces unnecessary friction between your intentions and your attention. One that recognizes your brain isn't a limitless machine, but a living system, vulnerable to fatigue, shaped by context, always responding to the cues around it.

Design, in this sense, isn't just aesthetic. It's functional. It's architectural. It's about shaping space, time, and habits in a way that makes focus more likely and overstimulation less inevitable.

And that design begins at the level of your surroundings.

If your phone is always within reach, your attention will always be partially somewhere else. If every flat surface in your home is covered in chargers, screens, or remotes, your brain will interpret rest as an opportunity to consume. If your desk is buried in tabs, wires, and alerts, your mind will scatter before the work begins.

These aren't judgments. They're observations. And they're reversible.

Your mind doesn't need to be walled off from the world; it just needs fewer invitations to leave the moment.

That's what brain-friendly design does. It lowers the activation energy for presence. It removes the default pathways to distraction. It offers gentle cues back to depth.

This might mean keeping your phone in another room for the first hour of the day. It might mean turning off your laptop and putting it away each evening, rather than letting it sit open on the kitchen table. It might mean creating one corner in your home where no screens are allowed, not as a rule, but as an offering.

It also means reconsidering how you manage transitions.

Our brains don't shift well between modes without friction. Going from deep work to a Zoom call to a scroll through your feed to making lunch fractures your attention in ways you feel but don't always name. You end the day tired, not because you did too much, but because you shifted too much.

A brain-friendly life gives transitions their own space. Five minutes of stillness between tasks. A walk before switching from work to parenting. A full pause, no screens, no updates, before bed. These aren't luxuries. They're neural resets.

Your brain doesn't want to multitask. It intends to complete one rhythm before beginning another. And your life, if you let it, can be shaped to support that.

Lighting matters. Sound matters. Time of day matters.

You don't need a silent retreat to protect your focus. You need to stop fighting your biology.

Most people ignore their natural peaks and troughs of energy because the digital world runs 24/7. But your brain still runs in pulses. It wants to go deep in the morning. It wants to rest in the afternoon. It wants to be quiet after dinner. When you ignore that cycle, you burn out not from effort, but from resistance.

So one of the most potent forms of design you can offer yourself is a schedule that respects your rhythms. Not rigidly, but realistically. Don't force deep work at 4 p.m. if you know your mind is already scattered. Don't schedule three back-to-back meetings without allowing for a break in between. Please don't ask your brain to be always on, and then wonder why it always feels off.

This, too, is design. Temporal architecture. Structuring time in a way that makes clarity possible again.

And then there's the information you consume.

A brain-friendly life doesn't mean shutting out the world. But it does mean being selective. Not every news update deserves your attention. Not every video needs to play in the background. Not every idea is worth holding in your head.

Design your inputs the way you'd design a diet, not with perfection, but with intention.

Curate your feeds. Not to avoid discomfort, but to reduce noise. Keep a list of writers, thinkers, and creators who stretch your mind without overwhelming it. Read slowly. Read things that take more than three minutes. Watch lectures instead of comment clips. Let yourself go deep, not because it's virtuous, but because it's healthier.

Your attention is not a wasteful byproduct of your productivity. It's the core of your experience. How you shape it, by what you invite into your space, your time, your mind, is the most foundational form of self-care you have.

A brain-friendly life doesn't always look impressive from the outside.

It might mean you take fewer calls. It might mean you answer messages more slowly. It might mean you spend more time staring out the window, letting your thoughts settle before jumping back into the current.

But from the inside, it feels different. You feel less pulled. You feel more anchored. You stop asking yourself, "Why can't I focus?" and start noticing: "I am focused, because I've made it possible to be."

And perhaps the most remarkable part? You start enjoying your mind again. Not because it's optimized. Not because it's always on task. But because it's yours. Not an inbox. Not a feed. Not a reaction engine. Just a mind. Spacious. Present. Designed to thrive, not survive. And in the right environment, it will.

Chapter 45: Tech and Intimacy

Intimacy doesn't disappear in a digital world; it changes shape. And often, it gets flattened.

You text instead of calling. You react with an emoji instead of responding with words. You check in via shared photos, watch a story, skim a status, and tell yourself that you're "keeping in touch." But over time, those moments begin to feel like contact without closeness. The more you reach, the more something essential slips between your fingers: presence.

Technology hasn't made us incapable of intimacy, but it has made us forget what real closeness requires. Not efficiency. Not constant communication. But sustained attention.

Intimacy is built not on volume, but on quality. It's the feeling of being fully seen, fully heard, entirely held, even for a few seconds. And no matter how smart our devices become, no app can simulate what it means to be *with* someone, not just adjacent to them on a screen.

We used to treat communication as an event. A letter. A phone call. A visit. Something with shape, something you prepared for and remembered afterward. Now it's ambient. Ongoing. Fragmented. You're always in contact, but rarely in communion.

This shift didn't happen because people changed. It happened because the infrastructure changed. Because the expectation of an immediate response replaced the possibility of a genuine response. Because algorithms began deciding which parts of a conversation you should see. Because the sheer ease of connection removed the friction that once made attention feel precious.

And now we're left in an intimacy paradox: we are more connected than ever, but lonelier in our relationships.

Not because we care less. But because the mechanisms of caring have been redefined. Reduced.

To rebuild intimacy in a digital world, we don't need to reject technology. We need to reclaim intentionality.

That begins with presence. It starts with a conscious decision, often made, that when you are with someone, you are *with* them.

That might mean turning the phone face down during dinner. It might mean letting a message sit unread so you can stay engaged in the conversation in front of you. It might mean saying no to multitasking on a video call. Not to prove a point, but to protect the container in which the connection grows.

Presence is not just about proximity. It's about being psychologically available. And when a screen is always within reach, that availability becomes diluted, sliced into smaller and smaller moments of partial attention.

Intimacy resists that slicing. It asks for your whole self.

And sometimes, giving that self means sitting in silence with someone. Sometimes it means listening without solving. Sometimes it means resisting the urge to document a moment to experience it.

Real intimacy isn't always efficient. It's often slow, awkward, and nonlinear. But in that slowness, trust deepens. You discover that not every meaningful exchange needs to be recorded. That the best moments are often the ones no one else sees. Love, friendship, and empathy all thrive in the unscanned, unshared spaces.

But the digital world rarely leaves those spaces unoccupied. Your time is always spoken for if you let it be. And that's why intimacy now must be protected, not because it's fragile, but because it's sacred.

Designating device-free zones isn't just about focus. It's about dignity. The dignity of undivided attention. Of saying to another human being: You are worth my presence. You are not background noise to my notifications.

And yes, there will be resistance. From others, from yourself. Because the habits of fragmentation run deep, but slowly, as the noise fades, something real begins to return. Eye contact that lasts. Laughter that lingers. Conversations that unfold instead of being trimmed into bullet points.

You remember what it's like not to be edited.

That's one of the quieter tragedies of digital life: we begin performing even in private. We curate our responses, delay our messages, and edit our thoughts before they've even been spoken.

And all that curation creates distance. Intimacy suffers not just from distraction, but from distortion.

To be close to someone, you have to risk being seen, not just filtered, not just optimized.

Technology can support that kind of vulnerability. A well-timed message can heal a rift. A shared playlist can say what words can't. A video call can sustain a long-distance friendship. But only when the tech serves the relationship, not the other way around.

So, ask yourself, gently, honestly: Is this tool helping us feel closer? Or just keeping us in touch?

Am I reaching out because I want to connect? Or because I'm afraid of being alone?

Am I replying out of love? Or out of habit?

There's no formula here. Just the slow, ongoing work of presence. Of showing up with your full attention, however imperfectly. Of letting the phone stay dark a little longer. Of choosing to linger instead of logging back on.

Because in the end, intimacy is not a function of connection speed.

It's a function of attention.

And no technology, no matter how advanced, can replace the simple, powerful act of choosing to be fully here with another human being.

Chapter 46: Raising Present Children in a Digital World

There is no perfect way to raise a child in the age of screens. No blueprint. No algorithm. No set of rules that will guarantee balance, resilience, and presence. Every parent knows this, or learns it quickly. What once felt simple now unfolds in a world where childhood itself is being reshaped by technology.

What has changed isn't just that screens are everywhere. It's that they are now woven into the daily rhythm of family life: the tablet handed over at dinner, the phone to quiet the tantrum, the constant background hum of YouTube, notifications, streaming shows designed not for narrative but for endless play. These are not signs of bad parenting. They are signs of a culture that has made digital immersion the path of least resistance.

But convenience has a cost. And the price isn't just time. It's attention. It's memory. It's the deep developmental work that happens not in entertainment, but in boredom, frustration, trial, and waiting.

To raise a present child in a digital world doesn't mean rejecting technology entirely. It means creating a space in which presence is possible. It means teaching, not just through limits, but through modelling, that attention is a finite and sacred thing.

Children learn more from what they see than what they're told. If the adults around them are perpetually distracted, scrolling while speaking, checking while listening, apologizing while glancing at the screen, the message is clear: presence is negotiable. Distraction is normal.

But when a child sees you put your phone away for no reason other than being *with* them, they learn something else: that attention is a gift, not a default, that a moment shared without interruption is worth protecting. That they don't need to perform or compete with a screen to feel seen.

That's where it starts, not with screen limits, but with values.

Ask yourself: What kind of inner world do I want my child to build?

Because the digital world offers stimulation, but rarely reflection, it provides content, but rarely depth. If children never learn to be bored, they never learn to imagine. If they never hear silence, they never learn to listen inward. If a screen instantly soothes every discomfort, they never learn to self-soothe.

But this isn't about becoming the "unplugged family." That ideal can be as performative and unrealistic as the one where everyone is fluent in the latest tech. Presence doesn't require perfection. It just asks for intention.

Maybe it means one screen-free meal a day. One afternoon a week, when nothing is scheduled or streamed. A bedtime routine without blue light. A weekend walk where phones stay home. Small things, repeated. Children don't need grand gestures. They need rhythms.

They also need boundaries that they don't have to enforce themselves.

We often expect kids to regulate their screen time before they've developed the tools to regulate anything else. Expecting a six-year-old to pause their favourite game, or a twelve-year-old to stop scrolling at bedtime, is like expecting them to say no to candy after you've handed them the whole bag.

Limits don't have to be punishment. They can be structured. They say: I care enough to create a space where you can grow without being constantly pulled away from yourself.

And still, there will be pushback. There will be friction. That's not failure. That's parenting in the real world. A world where tech companies have spent billions learning how to make their platforms irresistible, and where "just five more minutes" will never really mean five.

The goal isn't to win every battle. It's to build trust. To create an environment where your child knows that presence is something you value, and something you want to share with them.

And as they get older, that trust becomes more important than control.

You won't be able to monitor everything. You won't be able to stop every text, every notification, every influence. But if you've taught them how to pay attention, how to notice what drains them, what lifts them, what feels real, they will begin to make choices from that awareness.

You give them language, not laws.

Ask them: How do you feel after playing that game? What do you notice after an hour on TikTok? Does that chat make you feel more connected, or more anxious?

Not every conversation will lead to revelation. That's not the point. The point is to open a door, to help them build the habit of noticing. Because the greatest gift you can offer isn't control, it's discernment.

And maybe, as they grow, they'll remember what it felt like to have a quiet afternoon. To share a walk where nothing needed to be posted. To sit across from someone who looked them in the eyes and didn't glance away at a screen.

They may not say it. But it will stay with them. In the same way, your presence stays with you.

Because raising present children isn't about shielding them from the digital world, it's about giving them enough roots in the real one that they can navigate both.

Not with fear. Not with addiction. But with attention.

Chapter 47: Becoming an Intentional Consumer

It's easy to forget that consumption isn't just about things. Every day, you consume information, emotion, images, opinions, and stories. You absorb what you scroll past. You ingest more content in one day than previous generations encountered in a month. And most of it passes through your awareness without scrutiny.

That's not because you're careless. It's because the digital world is structured to bypass intention. It doesn't ask, "Would you like this?" It assumes you would. It shows you what it thinks you'll click before you've had the chance to think. And over time, that removes your sense of agency. You stop choosing. You receive.

In this kind of environment, intentional consumption becomes a radical act.

It means asking, every day, sometimes every hour, not just what you're watching, reading, or reacting to, but why. It means stepping away from the default and deciding what deserves space in your mind.

Because every bit of content leaves a trace.

A headline can shift your mood. A reel can pique your attention. A comment can echo for hours, subtly altering how you feel about yourself or others. Most of this happens beneath awareness. And yet the accumulation shapes you.

It shapes your sense of time because you measure it by the scroll.

It shapes your sense of self because you mirror what you repeatedly see.

It shapes your values because you begin to believe the loudest voices are the most important ones.

That's why intentional consumption isn't about cutting off the world. It's about curating what supports your inner life.

There is no one formula for that. Some people thrive on long-form articles, while others find restoration in music, or visual art, or carefully chosen podcasts. What matters isn't the medium. What matters is whether it expands your thinking or compresses it into something reactive, habitual, or numbing.

Most platforms don't encourage this kind of discernment. They optimize for stickiness. They feed you what you've already shown you'll click. They reward you for staying within a narrow loop. And so your job, as a consumer, becomes proactive: to move from passive to selective, from automatic to aware.

Start small. Begin by noticing what you consume that leaves you feeling more grounded, more human, more clear-minded. What voices help you think? What stories make you feel more connected to your real life, not less? What accounts, authors, and artists invite reflection instead of reaction?

These are the signals.

You don't need to unsubscribe from everything else overnight. But you can start tuning your feed, online and off, so that it reflects what you care about, not just what holds your gaze.

This applies to your physical environment, too. The books you keep visible. The shows you default to. The conversations you return to out of habit rather than meaning. Every piece of input either adds to your clarity or your confusion.

Over time, intentional consumption becomes less about control and more about rhythm. You build a cadence for absorbing information, one that respects your limits. You stop expecting yourself to keep up with everything. You let the algorithm feed someone else.

And perhaps most importantly, you get comfortable with less.

Fewer updates. Fewer opinions. Fewer loops. And in that quiet, you make room for something else: synthesis.

That's what gets lost in the noise, not just attention, but integration. When you consume less reactively, you have time to make meaning out of what you've seen. You notice patterns. You find resonance. You develop your perspective, rather than borrowing someone else's every time you open an app.

This is what it means to be not just a consumer, but a participant in your digital life.

You don't just take in what's offered. You shape what's allowed in.

And in doing so, you remember that your attention is not a public resource. It is yours to guard and to give.

That might mean unsubscribing. Muting. Logging off and letting a moment pass without capturing it. It might also mean following new voices, ones that challenge you, stretch you, remind you of a world beyond performance.

Intentional consumption is not austerity. It is a form of generosity to your future self. You choose now what kind of mind you want to carry forward. What thoughts will you repeat? What stories will you live inside?

And if that sounds abstract, try this: look at your feed right now. Scroll for one minute. Then ask, sincerely: Is this building the person I want to become?

If not, the change is yours to make, not by deleting everything, but by choosing what to amplify. That's the quiet revolution of this chapter. Not just consuming less. But consuming like it matters.

Because it does.

Chapter 48: Reclaiming Boredom, Curiosity, and Solitude

There was a time, not that long ago, when boredom was an everyday occurrence. You waited in line without a screen. You sat at red lights without checking anything. You spent whole afternoons with nothing in particular to do. These moments weren't thrilling, but they weren't meaningless either. They gave shape to the day. They gave your mind room to stretch.

Today, those empty spaces are almost gone.

They've been filled, not with purpose, but with noise. A spare moment becomes a scroll. A pause becomes a check-in. A quiet room becomes an invitation to "catch up." And the result isn't just overstimulation. It's the erosion of something older, softer, and necessary: the inner life.

To reclaim boredom, curiosity, and solitude is not to seek discomfort for its own sake. It's about returning to the conditions where your best thinking happens, where creativity takes root, where reflection becomes possible, where new ideas emerge from silence instead of from someone else's algorithm.

Boredom, for all its reputation, is not a flaw in the system. It is the system's reset function. It tells you when you've finished something. It prompts your mind to wander, to invent, to question. Children know this instinctively, until we train them to avoid it. But boredom is not a problem to fix. It's a space to inhabit.

In a screen-saturated world, boredom now arrives with discomfort. It feels wrong. Like wasted time. As though every empty moment must be filled, or else you've failed to keep up.

But stillness is not the absence of value. It is the environment in which value becomes visible.

To reclaim boredom means allowing yourself to be unproductive. To stare out the window. To go for a walk without headphones. To let your thoughts meander. Not because you're looking for insight, but because that meandering is the soil in which insight grows.

When your mind is constantly fed, it stops seeking. It becomes passive. It waits to be told what to think, what to feel, what to care about. But boredom activates something older than the feed. It draws your attention inward.

From that inwardness, curiosity is born.

Genuine curiosity doesn't come from clicking a headline. It doesn't come from being told what's trending. It comes from a quiet, internal "why?" or "what if?" It begins in wonder, not in content. And wonder requires space. It needs moments that haven't already been spoken for by pings and prompts and autoplay videos.

If you want to feel curious again, you have to let yourself get a little bored first.

Curiosity is not efficient. It resists the swipe. It lingers. It asks questions that don't have immediate answers. It makes you read one more page, even when the summary would have sufficed. It prompts you to ask someone a follow-up question instead of just liking their post.

In digital life, curiosity is one of the first things to flatten. You're presented with so much information, already filtered and categorized, that there's no need to go deeper. You become a consumer of surface, and surface is easy to abandon.

But when you reclaim curiosity, you remember how to follow a thought past its headline. You remember how to ask things that can't be Googled. You remember how it feels to be fascinated, not by what someone told you to care about, but by something your mind stumbled into.

Solitude is the third piece of this recovery.

Not loneliness. Not isolation. Solitude. The experience of being alone without being disconnected. Of sitting with yourself, not in avoidance, but in presence. And that's harder than it sounds in a world where your every idle moment can be filled.

To be alone now is a kind of resistance.

Because the second you feel yourself drifting inward, a voice inside says, "Check something." And if you do, the solitude disappears. Not just physically, but mentally. You are no longer with yourself. You are somewhere else, responding, reacting, curating.

Reclaiming solitude means refusing that reflex.

It means going for a walk and letting the silence settle. It means sitting in the passenger seat of a car without opening your phone. It means waking up and not reaching immediately for the day's digital noise.

Solitude gives shape to your thoughts. It lets you examine your own life without someone else's voice colouring it. And it gives you space to remember what you want, not what you've seen rewarded or reposted, but what feels real in your own body.

Without boredom, curiosity withers. Without curiosity, solitude becomes dull. Without solitude, your attention is never entirely your own.

Reclaiming these three doesn't mean retreating from the world. It means recovering your sense of agency within it.

And the path back is not grand. It is quiet. It begins with five minutes of stillness. A skipped scroll. A moment of reflection instead of reaction. And gradually, you remember: your mind is not a problem to solve. It is a place to inhabit.

This is where your clearest thoughts come from. Not from urgency. Not from updates. From space. From slowness. From silence.

Chapter 49: The Self Beyond the Scroll

Who are you when no one is watching? What happens when there's nothing to post, nothing to check, no comments to respond to, or updates to deliver? Who are you when the performance pauses?

It's a question fewer of us ask now, not because it's unimportant, but because the scroll never really stops. The feed has become a mirror, and like all mirrors, it demands a particular posture. We shape ourselves in response to it. The angles we share. The versions we emphasize. The stories we tell are not just about events, but about who we are.

Over time, these choices accumulate. And subtly, quietly, the self becomes flattened, optimized for visibility rather than depth.

This isn't unique to social media. It's a function of being constantly seen. When attention becomes a form of currency, there's always an incentive to refine, to manage, to prove. But that incentive draws you outward. And the more time you spend projecting a version of yourself, the more difficult it becomes to hear the quieter voice inside, the one that doesn't care about metrics, the one that doesn't announce its worth.

This is the self beyond the scroll. The part of you that doesn't exist for an audience.

You can't access it through speed. You can't optimize your way toward it. You find it, or rediscover it, in the moments that aren't captured, when the phone is off. When you're walking alone and no one knows where you are. When you're doing something, not for validation, but for its strange joy.

For some, it's painting. For others, cooking without a photo is a challenge. Sitting in a park with a notebook. Reading an entire book without telling anyone. Calling someone just because you thought of them, not because it's their birthday.

These moments don't ask to be shared. They ask to be lived.

And that's the shift: from performance to presence, from managing an identity to inhabiting one.

The scroll isn't evil. It's just endless. It will never tell you to stop. It will never say: "That's enough now. Go live." And so the burden falls to you, to know when to close the window. When to trust that your life, lived privately, is no less meaningful for being unseen.

It may be more so.

Because the private self is where your values are practiced, not proclaimed. It's where your integrity lives, not in what you say, but in what you choose when no one else is watching. It's where your attention returns after the performance ends.

When you don't pause to reconnect with that part of yourself, you begin to confuse exposure for intimacy, visibility for identity. You start to measure your worth by how you interact with others. And slowly, your interior life atrophies, not because you meant to lose it, but because you stopped feeding it.

Recovering that life takes time. And gentleness. And space.

You begin, perhaps, by doing one thing each day that doesn't get posted. A thought you keep for yourself. A walk you don't track. A moment you let pass without trying to frame it.

It's not about hiding. It's about sovereignty.

The self beyond the scroll doesn't need to hide, because it doesn't need to explain. It is not a secret. It is simply whole. And it reminds you that you do not have to be witnessed to be real.

This might feel unfamiliar at first. You may notice a pull, almost like withdrawal. A part of you wants to share, to check, to affirm that the moment mattered. That you mattered.

But that pull weakens the more you meet it with presence instead of reaction. The more you resist turning every experience into content, the more you begin to experience your life again, not as a series of shareable moments, but as a continuous thread, deeply felt.

Eventually, that becomes enough.

Not in the minimalistic sense, not as a trade-off, but as a quiet wholeness. You find joy in solitude, curiosity without commentary, and creativity that doesn't need applause.

The scroll will still be there. But you will no longer be *in* it. You'll dip in, not dive. You'll observe, not absorb. And from that distance, the performance loses its grip. You start making choices that align with who you are, not just who you want to be seen as.

Because that's the real promise of digital clarity, not just less distraction, but more selfhood. Not just quiet.

But truth.

152

Chapter 50: The Reboot Is Permanent

This is not a detox.

You are not "stepping away" for a short time in hopes of snapping back refreshed, only to return to the same patterns, the same noise, the same silent erosion of your focus and peace. This is not a cleanse. Not a challenge. Not a break.

It is a turning point.

The reboot is permanent, not because you will never use your devices again, but because you now see them differently. You have stepped outside the cycle long enough to understand it, not as an inevitability, but as a construct. One you can revise.

You're not just quitting habits. You're reclaiming authorship.

That's what this entire journey has been about. Not subtraction for its own sake, but restoration. Of presence. Of boundaries. Of a mind that belongs, once again, to you.

The digital world is not going anywhere. Nor should it. Your tools are still helpful. Your platforms still serve a purpose. But they are no longer your habitat. You no longer live *in* them, nor do you mistake their urgency for your own.

This shift is subtle and radical. It doesn't announce itself in dramatic gestures. It shows up in the smallest places.

You feel your body relax when you set your phone down instead of checking one more thing. You wake without reaching for a screen. You go to bed with thoughts that are your own, not absorbed from someone else's reel. You find yourself less reactive, less scattered, less consumed by the endless scroll of other people's lives.

You're not unreachable. You're just less interrupted.

This isn't a retreat from the world, it's a re-entry into it. With more clarity. More rhythm. More room to breathe.

You've remembered how to be here. Not passively consuming experience, but actively inhabiting it. Not seeing every pause as a productivity gap, but as part of the architecture of attention.

This is your new foundation.

And because it's built on awareness, not rigidity, it can flex with your life. You can adapt it. Expand it. Return to it, again and again, without shame. You now have the language to notice when the noise begins to creep back in. You can feel the moment your attention starts to fray. And you can respond, not by blaming yourself, but by adjusting the structure around you.

Because the point of this reboot was never purity.

It was permission.

Permission to disconnect without guilt. To rest without explanation. To protect your time, your energy, your presence, not as a luxury, but as a necessity for living a life that feels like yours.

You now know how to recognize the difference between use and compulsion. Between communication and performative contact. Between creativity and constant consumption. That knowledge is yours to keep. It does not expire.

And if you forget, because you will, you also now know how to begin again. Not from scratch, but from understanding. You've done the work of interruption. You've remembered that attention is not a reflex, but a decision.

So let your digital life move forward from here, not with fear, not with rules, but with intention.

Let your devices be tools again. Let your feeds be silent when you want silence. Let your worth be measured by something more profound than the frequency of your responses.

Let your mind be yours. You don't need to escape the digital world. You need to stop dissolving into it. You are allowed to pause. You are permitted to go quiet. You are allowed to make this the beginning of something permanent, not because you have to, but because you can.

You have rebooted. You are awake. You are home.

Trilogy Epilogue

You didn't need a new app.

You didn't need a better routine, or a smarter productivity hack, or another reason to feel like you weren't doing enough.

What you needed, and maybe didn't know you were allowed to ask for, was space. Space to think again. To feel again. To remember what a quiet mind feels like when the world's noise isn't constantly summoning it.

This trilogy began with a question most of us were too distracted to articulate:

What happened to my attention?

From there, we followed that thread, through multitasking myths, burnout cycles, and overstimulated digital landscapes, to something more profound. Something slower. A path of return.

You've now rebuilt the architecture of your day. You've examined what drains you, what drives you, and what defines your time. And now, at the end of this book, and the end of this trilogy, you stand in a different kind of space: the one where you *choose* what your life will hold.

That is the hidden power behind all these pages. Not perfection. Not controlled. But clarity. The kind that doesn't demand urgency, because it understands presence. The kind that doesn't fear stillness, because it has practiced it. The kind that sees focus not as a task to master, but as a way to belong entirely to your own life.

This isn't the end of the conversation. It's the beginning of a new one, with yourself, with your attention, with the kind of world you want to help build. A world where wholeness isn't something you chase in the margins of your schedule. It's something you live from.

A world where your energy serves your values. Where your time reflects your true priorities, and where your devices don't define your day, *you* do.

You've reclaimed your attention. You've rebuilt your rhythms. You've rebooted your mind.

Now go live accordingly.

THE DEEP WORK SOCIETY

Volume 1: The Myth of Multitasking
Volume 2: The Burnout Blueprint
Volume 3: The Digital Reboot

About the Author

Written anonymously by a former multitasker who lived the burnout, bought the productivity tools, and still couldn't hear himself think.

The Deep Work Society trilogy was created not to impress, but to invite. Each book is a quiet rebellion against the noise—offered by someone who stepped back, paid attention, and started writing things down.

No name. No brand. Just ideas that might help you remember what it feels like to be present again.

About the Publisher

Welcome to The Book On Publishing

At The Book On Publishing, we believe in rewriting the rules of learning. Whether you're chasing your next big idea, building a better life, or simply curious about what should have been taught in school, you've come to the right place.

We're a platform built for dreamers, doers, and lifelong learners—offering bold, practical books and tools that empower you to take charge of your journey. From real-world skills to mindset mastery, we publish the book on what matters.

No fluff. No lectures. Just what you need to know, delivered with clarity, purpose, and a spark of curiosity.

Start exploring. Start growing. Start writing your story.

Read more at https://thebookon.ca.

Acknowledgment of AI Assistance

Portions of this book were developed with the support of ChatGPT, an AI language model created by OpenAI. While every word has been carefully reviewed and refined by the author, ChatGPT served as a valuable tool for brainstorming, editing, and structuring ideas. Its assistance helped accelerate the creative process and bring clarity to complex topics.

www.ingramcontent.com/pod-product-compliance
Lightning Source LLC
Chambersburg PA
CBHW071625030726

47598CB00001B/435